PACIFIC ELECTRIC

RAILWAY

VOLUME TWO - THE EASTERN DIVISION

COVINA LINE — POMONA LINE — SAN BERNARDINO LINE — RIVERSIDE LINE — FREIGHT SERVICE
RAILWAY POST OFFICE SERVICE — BOX MOTOR SERVICE
POMONA LOCAL LINES — RIVERSIDE-CORONA LOCAL LINE — SAN BERNARDINO-REDLANDS LOCAL LINES

Compiled by Donald Duke

Golden West Books

PACIFIC ELECTRIC RAILWAY

Volume Two
The Eastern Division

Published by Golden West Books
San Marino, California 91118 U.S.A.

Library of Congress Catalog Card No. 2001-1040640
I.S.B.N. No. 0-87095-117-3

Library of Congress Cataloging-in-Publication Data

Duke, Donald, 1929-
Pacific Electric Railway / compiled by Donald Duke.
p. cm.
Includes bibliographical references.
Contents: v. 2. The Eastern Division.
1. Pacific Electric Railway Company. 2. Street railroads—California, Southern. I. Title.

TF727.P4 D85 2001
388.4'6'097949—dc21 2001-1040640

COVER ILLUSTRATION

Rolling along on private right-of-way, near La Verne, a three car Pomona bound interurban train skips along through the orange groves. At La Verne, the train will head south direct to Pomona. The date was 1937 when the area was full of orange trees. Today it is all tract houses. — Charles D. Savage

TITLE PAGE ILLUSTRATION

You can almost hear the whine of the heavy traction motors as electric locomotive No. 1591 was photograped, in 1941, switching around PE's San Bernardino yard. A gondola car of scrap metal and an old wood box car are being taken to the Santa Fe interchange. — Jack Whitmeyer

Golden West Books

P.O. Box 80250 • San Marino, California • 91118-8250

Gordon Jackson and Harold Stewart at the
Pasadena Carbarn, Stewart is the man at the right.

This volume is dedicated
to Harold Stewart
Pacific Electric photographer,
motorman, and friend.

LINES OF THE PACIFIC ELECTRIC RAILWAY IN SOUTHERN CALIFORNIA

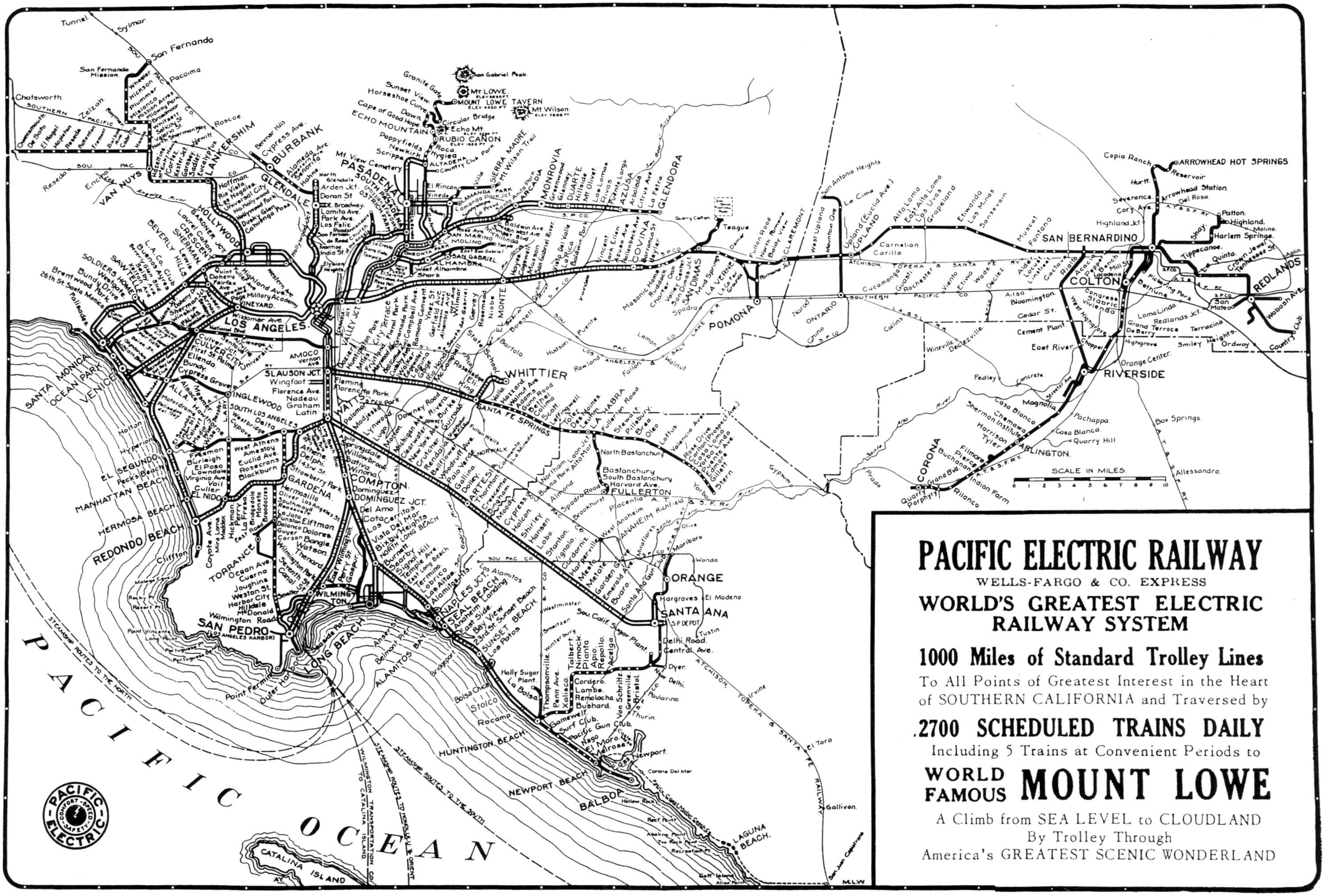

Pacific Electric interurban car No. 1028, one of two cars assigned to the "Orange Empire Trolley Trip," paused in the orange groves near Covina. The daily trip covered over 150 miles through the heart of the greatest orange growing section of the world. No visit to Southern California was complete without having viewed, at close range, the endless glories of the Kingdom of the Orange. The tour conductor, standing next to the car did not wear the customary PE uniform. — DONALD DUKE COLLECTION

Table of Contents

Note: The bracketed figures are the page numbers for the series of volumes one and two. The unbracketed figures are for the volume you are holding or Volume Two.

On a railroad enthusiast special train, car No. 1243, clears the crossing at Claremont. The motorman was Robert Slocum who was a railroad enthusiast to boot. You will notice the front of the car was jammed with people which was customary on such trains. — Robert Slocum

Introduction

Henry Edwards Huntington was Collis P. Huntington's favorite nephew, and he established Henry in all kinds of adventures. He was president of the Newport Shipbuilding & Drydock Company, vice president of Chesapeake & Ohio Railroad, and various other offices. Collis was two generations older than Henry, and held the position of one the "Big Four" of the Central Pacific, and ended up as chairman of the Southern Pacific Company. Collis appointed Henry as an associate vice president of the Southern Pacific Company. He was being groomed to take over the helm of the Southern Pacific on the death of Collis.

At the turn of the century, Henry was a middle-aged man who had distinguished himself in the railroad business. Many believed that he would retire in luxury and philanthropy. Henry was a builder by nature, he invested in electric railways and was involved with the original Market Street Railway of San Francisco. Henry's 30 year association with his uncle was undoubtedly instrumental in shaping his career in building the Pacific Electric system in Southern California, and the development of the Huntington Land & Improvement Company, the real estate arm of Huntington's interests. In 1898 he purchased the Los Angeles Railway, the street car system operating in central Los Angeles. He immediately extended the company's lines with the financial efforts of his friend Isaias W. Hellman, a prominent banker of Los Angeles and San Francisco.

On August 13, 1900, Collis P. Huntington died. It appeared obvious that Henry would attain his dream and succeed his mentor as president and chairman of the Southern Pacific. It was quickly learned that Collis had been short of cash and placed $300,496.00 worth of capital stock of the Southern Pacific as collateral with a large banking firm in New York. The firm, not wishing to be holding the sack, approached Edward Harriman and asked if he wished to pick up the shares of Southern Pacific stock? Harriman always wanted to own a transcontinental railroad system. He picked up the SP stock, and together with his Union Pacific holdings, nearly had a railroad from coast to coast.

Harriman was already on the board of the Southern Pacific, and when he announced at the 1900 board of directors meeting that he had control, Henry saw his dream die. The board was unwilling to see the influence of another Huntington as president of the Southern Pacific. Harriman asked Huntington to remain on the board of the Southern Pacific, which he did. When the estate of Collis P. Huntington was settled Henry would receive half of his estate, and Collis's wife Arabella would receive the other half, as well as their Park Avenue home. Henry was a wealthy man. He sold his interests in electric railways around San Francisco and moved to Los Angeles. He virtually invested in and developed metropolitan Los Angeles and Southern California.

The Pacific Electric Railway was incorporated November 10, 1901 and Epes Randolph, the civil engineer of the Yuma Division of Southern Pacific was recruited to head up Henry Huntington's interest. Randolph can truly be classified as the architect of the Pacific Electric, with Henry providing the money, and more or less a father figure. At the time Henry was spending a great deal of time in New York. It was Randolph's influence that the Pacific Electric was built standard gauge, rather than a narrow-gauge interurban line.

At the time Southern California was so vast and its population so dispersed, Huntington believed the only way to tie everything together was by an interurban electric railway stystem. He invested heavily in the San Gabriel, Pomona and San Bernardino valleys. In order to exploit Riverside's colorful past, Huntington invested heavily in Frank Miller's Glenwood Tavern (later to become the famous Riverside Mission Inn). He invested in orange groves in and around Riverside, and vineyards around San Bernardino. Huntington played a more direct role of regional booster. Bringing new industry to Southern California, and advising newcomers of the sunshine and water availability. In 1903 he set up a felt factory at the western edge of Alhambra, and inviting his boyhood friend from Onteonta, New York, Alfred Dolge, to set up a business in the old Shorb Winery building.

The political cartoons of the day, which were on the editorial page of the *Los Angeles Times*, were not always favorable to Henry E. Huntington. The *Times* claimed Huntington was about to create a monopoly of public transportation.

The town became known as Dolgeville.

The tremendous period of interurban railway construction began in 1902, the *Street Railway Journal* for May 7, 1902 had this to say: "The Pacific Electric Monrovia Line will undoubtedly be pushed east to Azusa, Glendora, and then on to Pomona. The sale of Mr. Huntington's interests in San Francisco street railways placed large sums of money at his disposal for Southern California building. It has been announced that Henry E. Huntington is to construct a belt line from Los Angeles to Whittier, Riverside, Redlands, San Bernardino, Ontario, Pomona, and then back to Los Angeles. The new line will be four tracks throughout, two for freight, and two for passenger service." After initiating most of the Pacific Electric routes, Epes Randolph came down with tuberculous, and returned to the dry desert air of the Southern Pacific Yuma Division. Huntington then appointed Charles E. Graham, president of Southern Pacific's Pacific Improvement Company to take charge of the growing Pacific Electric Railway.

As the Pacific Electric network grew, and when the Monrovia Line was completed March 1, 1903 (see Volume One), many towns in the eastern section of the San Gabriel Valley saw the line's extension to Covina closer to realization. Covina citizens organized a committee which began acquiring a right-of-way for an electric line, acting on the personal assurances that he would build the PE to Covina. Along with Charles E. Graham, Huntington believed a more direct route to Covina would be best, rather than run down south from Monrovia. An extension from the junction of the Pasadena Short Line and Alhambra Line, along the route of the narrow-gauge San Gabriel Valley Rapid Transit was considered. The proposed route from a point called Covina Junction (later called Valley Junction), would be about 12 miles long.

Unfortunately for Henry E. Huntington, his burgeoning electric railway network placed him on a direct collision course with the powerful Edward H. Harriman. As each new Pacific Electric line opened, the Southern Pacific line serving the same general vacinity had to cut back on local passenger service. Huntington's Los Angeles Railway had become highly profitable and was destroying the other traction properties with its extensions. In April 1903, all the properties of the Los Angeles Traction Company, which was part street car and interurban, passed into the possession of Senator William A.Clark, the copper king of Montana. Clark was building the third transcontinental line to Los Angeles known as the San Pedro, Los Angeles & Salt Lake Railroad.

Clark needed feeder routes into the Southern California region to provide his new line with passengers and freight. Clark had an alliance with the Union Pacific and Harriman. Harriman now controlled the Union Pacific and Southern Pacific as one single line. The May 2, 1903 *Street Railway Journal* has this to say: "Many believe that Senator Clark, in entering the electric railway field in Los Angeles, and Southern California, is backed by Edward H. Harriman, president of the Southern Pacific. Such a syndicate would compete with Henry E. Huntington's system, the Los Angeles Railway and the Pacific Electric Railway, for supremacy of the electric railway traffic of Southern California."

Wherever the Pacific Electric cars went, subdividers and growth quickly followed. Harriman agreed that Huntington's electric system which ran interurban cars more frequently and faster, would completely undercut Southern Pacific's passenger business in Southern California. Pacific Electric's building program was expensive. Isaias W. Hellman who had a large financial stake in the Los Angeles Railway and the Pacific Electric Railway asked Huntington when dividends would be forthcoming? Huntington plowed all income back into his lines. Huntington became aroused that Hellman might bolt and Harriman might put his foot down. Huntington resigned his long time vice presidency and board member of the Southern Pacific.To find out what Harriman would do, Huntington accelerated interurban construction and then announced that the PE would extend to Santa Barbara and San Diego. So set the state for the showdown.

The battle lines were drawn and it quickly became known that Edward H. Harriman was the winner. Isaias W. Hellman became a Judas, and sold out Huntington by selling Harriman 50 percent interest in the Pacific Electric Railway. Hellman did not have the guts to offer Huntington a chance to pickup his interests. Huntington felt betrayed, and rightly he should be. He immediately went to San Francisco to confront Harriman. Huntington went to Harriman's office, and was kept waiting for two hours. When Harriman's door opened, who should step out in the company but Isaias W. Hellman. Huntington said nothing, and went into Harriman's office.

It was now the Huntington-Harriman Syndicate. Harriman stated he had greater things on his mind than to battle Huntington over his extensions of the Pacific Electric. There were heavy snow problems on Donner Pass, and the Colorado River was running wild and flooding the Imperial Valley (the nation's bread basket)

Just like today, not everyone was enthusiastic about Henry E. Huntington's Pacific Electric Railway and his power company the Pacific Light & Power Company. If Huntington was building something, there was always a group of citizens against him.

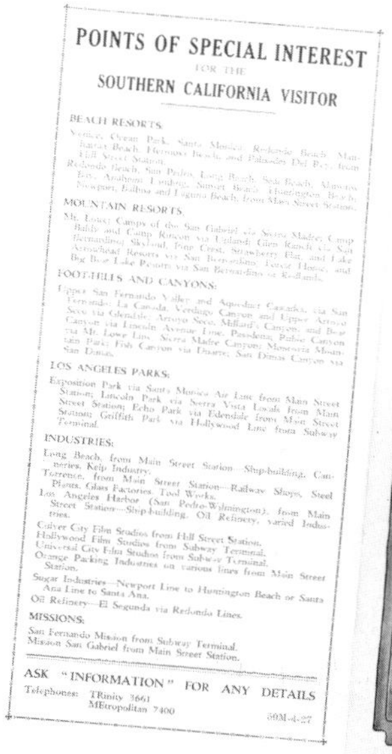

The Pacific Electric was famous for its "Orange Empire Trolley Trip." The route was from Los Angeles to Rialto, down to Riverside, back up to San Bernardino, and then to Redlands. Cost of the day trip was $4.00. — DONALD DUKE COLLECTION

with water. Harriman said he would closely ally with the Pacific Electric, and as a hand of friendship, would sell the Los Angeles Traction Company line to Huntington's Los Angeles Railway. He also declared that Huntington would remain in absolute control over the destinies of his Pacific Electric, however, Harriman was now a heavy investor in PE, and his voice would go far in influencing future construction decisions.

Although Edward H. Harriman did not live long enough to gain complete control over the Pacific Electic, he did veto the projected lines to Santa Barbara and San Diego. Later in 1903, Huntington, on his own, acquired the Ontario Electric Company which operated the Ontario & San Antonio Heights Railway, and also the San Bernardino Gas & Electric Company, which ran local transportation in San Bernardino and Redlands. He also invested heavily in the San Bernardino Valley Traction Company and the Riverside & Arlington Railway. Riverside, some 50 miles from downtown Los Angeles, believed that Huntington would connect Riverside with Los Angeles with his Pacific Electric Railway.

On June 6, 1903, Huntington and friends incorporated the Los Angeles Inter-Urban Railway which would build the line from Covina Junction to Covina. The LAI-U would build lines to La Habra, Redlands, Riverside, San Bernardino, Riverside, Santa Ana, and into the San Fernando Valley. Initially the LAI-U was wholly owned by Huntington and friends, and completely independent of the Pacific Electric and influence of the Southern Pacific. However, in time the LAI-U became an appendage of the Pacific Electric. Because Huntington had retained many interurban lines in his own name, he was able to transfer these holdings to the LAI-U. In June 1904 the LAI-U assumed control of two more Huntington-owned lines the Riverside & Arlington, and the Santa Ana & Orange Motor road, a steam dummy line.

Most of the Pacific Electric Railway lines were extended into areas that were unsettled and would grow. Several were built into areas where Henry E. Huntington had large land holdings. Under the leadership of his lawyer George S. Patton, the father of the famous General George S. Patton, Jr., the Huntington Land & Improvement Company was organized to sell plots of land for homes and businesses. Most of the land was sold through agents and Huntington's name was never mentioned. The Huntington Library has a list of some 45 land agents. The only place land was sold by the Huntington Land & Improvement Company was in San Marino. Now let us extend the line from Covina Junction to the town of Covina.

On June 30, 1907, the double track Covina Line was open for service. Interurban cars entered the town of Covina on Badillo Street, which wasn't paved at the time. Charles S. Lawrence, the Pacific Electric's official photographer, framed car No. 423 alongside a grove of eucalyptus trees. Note that the train crew wore frocked coats at the time, and their caps were white. — CHARLES D. SAVAGE

Covina Rail Line

Interurban cars Nos. 1028-1029 were specially fitted up to serve the Orange Empire Trolley Trip. The cars had fewer seats so there was leg room for the day trip. Otherwise the cars were a typical 1000-class car. — Donald Duke Collection

On July 21, 1904, George E. Pillsbury, chief engineer of the Pacific Electric gave an interview to the *Los Angeles Times*. He said: "You may say that the next project of the Pacific Electric will be the line to Covina. The right-of-way will begin at Covina Junction and extend over the right-of-way of the former line of the San Gabriel Valley Rapid Transit which commenced at Aliso Street in Los Angeles and extended to Monrovia by way of Alhambra. This route was purchased by PE some time ago and will form a short line to Covina, Pomona, and eventually extend to towns further east."

The acquisition of the valuable right-of-way of the old San Gabriel Valley Rapid Transit was one of the first, and certainly one of the most valuable results of the understanding with Edward H. Harriman under the Los Angeles Inter-Urban Railway. The San Gabriel Valley Rapid Transit was the idea of the developer of Monrovia, William N. Monroe, a former civil engineer for the Southern Pacific in Texas and New Mexico. He designed a water level route from Monrovia to downtown Los Angeles in late 1887. He built a single track narrow-gauge from Monrovia to the east side of the Los Angeles River at Aliso Street. The collapse of the great land boom in 1888 made operation of the line unprofitable. It was then leased for two years by the Los Angeles Terminal Railway and converted to standard gauge. They desired the line because of the citrus packing houses along the route. The Southern Pacific acquired the line in 1894. On May 12, 1904, the SP sold and conveyed the line from Los Angeles to Alhambra to the Los Angeles Inter-Urban Railway.

Preliminary engineering work was done on the line to Covina beginning at Covina Junction and extended east to Ramona, where the old SGVRT right-of-way swung north through Alhambra, San Marino, to Monrovia. The single track line was converted to double-track and ballasted. Chief Engineer Pillsbury met with the Covina right-of-way committee. They drove over the whole right-of-way obtained by the committee before acceptance. It would not be long before construction would begin. In June 1904 construction camps were set up at Covina and El Monte. Surveys were made, rails ordered, and bridge construction begun. From Ramona the right-of-way would be a straight shoot to Covina.

Henry E. Huntington returned from New York aboard his private railroad car *San Marino* on July 10. The private car once belonged to uncle Collis P. Huntington and was called *Oneonta*, after their home town in New York. Henry changed the name to honor his new home in San Marino. His first act in returning was to authorize orders to start construction on the new Covina Line. For some unknown reason construction of the double track line just crawled along. Then on April 18, 1906 the great San Francisco earthquake and fire took place. It was June 1906 before things got under way once more. Additional grading camps were established at Covina Junction, Ramona, west of El Monte, and west of Covina. The Covina camp employed some 360 men who were operating graders with 300 horses. By July 2, 9.5 miles were graded, ballasted, ties laid out on the 11.6 mile route. Grading was to be completed by September 1906.

Covina was the name given to the subdivision of La Puente Rancho in the late 1880's. The region was a vineyard before the orange trees were planted. The name Covina means "a place of vines. "

Elias J. "Lucky" Baldwin gave some 50 acres of land across his ranch east of El Monte. In honor of Baldwin the

Pacific Electric named a stop after him. The town built around the station was known as Vineland until 1912 and was renamed Baldwin Park, former owner of the Puente de San Gabriel rancho, on which the city is situated. Over the whole line east of Ramona, grades were easy, long, with compensating short curves. With very little development along the route and the absence of crossing, this assured high-speed operation. Wood interurban cars of the California-type (half open, half closed) were tentatively to make the Los Angeles to Covina run in 45 minutes. There were two large trestles on the route. One, some 700 feet long across the San Gabriel River, and another 600 feet long over the Rio Hondo, a roaring river when it rained in the San Gabriel mountains. The heaviest grade was encountered just west of El Monte, where the grade had to be built up in order to get up and over the Rio Hondo.

Huntington, and chief engineer Pillsbury, were guests of the Covina Railroad Committee at the Covina Country Club on August 10, 1906. Following lunch the committee and PE officials inspected the construction work. Huntington revealed that rail laying would begin about August 14th at a point four miles west of Covina. He predicted that electric cars would start running in late December or the first part of 1907. Evidence that Covina Line construction was underway was that 15 carloads of steel rails had arrived at Port Los Angeles, with 42 more carloads expected later in the year. Bear in mind that at this time, rails had to arrive by ship around Cape Horn. The Panama Canal was in process of construction.

With ties in place, rail laying began at Vineland (Baldwin Park). A steam locomotive was leased from the Southern Pacific to handle the work trains during rail laying and overhead construction. Rail laying, and construction, more

Before the Covina Line opened for service, portions of the line were still single track. A 400 class car is out on the line testing starts and stops. The route was double track when opened on June 30, 1907. — Charles S. Lawrence

When the Covina Line opened in 1907, a Los Angeles bound train takes the curve at Ramona (now a part of Alhambra). The Ramona substation was off to the left in the trees. This was part of the Edgeware Square Real Estate tract. Note the wide open spaces at the time, which are now full of houses. The tract went belly-up during the depression and became a section of Alhambra. — Henry E. Huntington Library

A three-car train of 1200-class cars pulls alongside the Covina station with a load of commuters. You can hardly see the motorman, but he is to the left in the window. — Duke Middleton Collection

or less came to a halt as all crews where thrown into the battle to control the break in the Colorado River in the Imperial Valley. The Pacific Electric provided some 500 men to the project. Following the San Francisco fire and earthquake, everything was thrown into the effort to save the Imperial Valley. Trainload after trainload of rock and boulders were taken from Los Angeles to the Imperial Valley. The Salton Sea, a dry lake had grown into a monster. The Southern Pacific had raised their main line from Indio to Yuma three times higher up on the side of the valley. The Colorado River had to be stopped. After many attempts to plug the hole by bridging the gap and dumping of rock, the hole was finally plugged February 10, 1906. It would take three months to get crews back to their regular job working on the Covina Line. On October 21, 1906, the Covina *Argus* reported: "The last spike was driven yesterday (October 20th), on the first track of the Pacific Electric's Covina Line. It is believed that the new line will be ready for passengers before the first of the year. Scarcity of men working on the break of the Colorado River and lateness of materials have greatly delayed construction. As it is, only a single track had been constructed and that only from Vineland to Covina. The Pacific Electric is seriously considering rushing the completion of a single-track all the way to Los Angeles in order to permit the opening of the road as a single-track line to favor Covina residents."

The press reported on November 10, 1906, that the Pacific Electric was running tests between Covina and Vineland, and the whole line should be in running order by February 1st. The only trouble was that the bridge over the San Gabriel River would take some weeks to finish. In June 1907 track crews were diverted to Pomona to finish three miles of local line trackage, otherwise the PE would lose its franchise. Later in the month the final grooming of the single track line became double-track.

Finally, on June 30, 1907, the Covina Line was finished and ready for service. The date was set for July 1, and the featured event was a town barbecue. People from all over the valley were invited and an estimated 5,000 people

In 1939, car No. 1200 rolls east along Badillo Street in Covina. This single car interurban is bound for Riverside. These cars had a toilet at opposite ends of each car. — CHARLES D. SAVAGE

Interurban car No. 1227 rolls east along Badillo Street, in 1946, as it nears the civic center of Covina. — BILL EVERETT COLLECTION

stuffed themselves and took free rides on "P.E. Day" in Covina. The whole Covina Line was double-track, cars ran east and west on Badillo Street. A small ordinary station was built at Badillo and Covina Avenue. From the station in the center of town, an additional 2.58 miles of single track ran east and ended in a small yard. The only other actual station on the line was at El Monte, where the PE crossed the main line of the Southern Pacific.

Most of the other passenger stops were a flat mound of dirt or gravel, some containing a bench on which to wait for the next interurban. Larger stops in small towns contained a roofed shelter. The PE had to build a control tower at El Monte to stop their trains in case a Southern Pacific passenger or freight train came along. Since the PE was the last railroad to cross the SP line, it was up to them to install the crossing control to protect interurban trains.

Single car No. 1227 rolls along Badillo Street headed for the Covina station during October 1946. (LEFT) Car No. 1227 leaves the Covina station bound for San Bernardino. — Ivan Baker - Craig Rasmussen Collection

On November 1, 1941, all service was cut back to Baldwin Park, except for several rush hour trains to Covina. Had the Pacific Electric held off abandoning the line east of Baldwin Park until after December 7, 1941, the PE would have been a godsend to those in the Riverside and San Bernardino areas. In this scene at Baldwin Park, a turnaround train pulls up to the shelter at Baldwin Park to pick up a load of passengers. All service was discountinued to Covina on March 28, 1947. All service was discontinued on the San Bernardino Line on October 15, 1947. — Robert Slocum

As World War II traffic hit Southern Pacific Golden State-Sunset Route, traffic in and out of Los Angeles stacked up. Being that Southern Pacific was a single track railroad, except for passing sidings, it became necessary that something had to be done. Pacific Electric's San Bernardino Line became a second main line between Los Angeles and Colton. Using steam locomotives, together with electric locomotives to operate the overhead contact signals and wig wag crossing signals, such operations became the norm. Covina did not like the smoky steam locomotives operating on their city street, and passed an ordinance against their use. The only alternative was to use Southern Pacific's branch line which ran north of town as a roundabout route. PE electrified the branch from Baldwin Park to San Dimas. This is a view of the Covina station north of the City of Covina. — Harold Stewart

The original Covina Line was powered with 600 volts in the overhead wire. Substations were located at Covina Junction, Ramona, and Vineland. It would be some time before the line would be converted to a 1,200 volt system.

The Covina *Argus* in February 1907 stated that 50 new cars has been acquired from the St. Louis Car company for the Covina Line. These interurban cars were of the latest design and equipped with the latest electrical equipment. They had multiple-unit control which enabled the motorman on the lead car to operate all cars in the train. The open section, which was without windows had electric heaters running along the inside so the feet could be kept warm. The outside seats, instead of having lattice work sides, were solid to the elbow rest. Curtains were provided which could be pulled down in case of rain. The new cars were given Nos. 800-850.

Not all 800-class interurban cars were used on the Covina Line, only a few. These fast cars were used on the Santa Ana, Long Beach, and San Pedro lines. Electric cars were far superior to steam operated trains, and were ideal for short haul traffic. They had quicker starting and stopping ability, were run in shorter trains and more often, and had the ability to run over downtown Los Angeles streets which took passengers closer to where they wanted to go. Now on to San Dimas and Pomona.

Three 1600-class electric locomotives idle away at SP's Covina station waiting for a helper run east or west. Usually steam was applied to freights going east at State Street Yard, with an electric on the point, or behind the steam power. Electric locomotives with trolley poles were necessary to activate signals and wig wags. — Bill Everett Collection

Pomona Line

In the late 1940's, No. 1214 heads a four-car train of 1200-class interurban cars along Garey Avenue, bound for Los Angeles. The train has just crossed the Union Pacific main line and the station may be seen at the left. — RALPH MELCHING

Henry E. Huntington had many land interests in, and around, Pomona. It was the largest town between Los Angeles and San Bernardino, and expanded after the arrival of the Southern Pacific. The area was full of orange groves and vineyards, hence the town developed early. Before Huntington arrived there were several local street car systems in the town. There was the Pomona Street Railway (steam dummy line), and four horse car lines such as the Second Street Railroad, the Holt & San Antonio Avenue Street Railway, the Orange Grove Street Railway, and the Pomona Heights Street Railroad. Citizens urged Huntington to connect Pomona with his fast interurban system.

Huntington's outlay of capital in Southern California, and the Pacific Electric in such a short time, provided the impetus that propelled the region into a cultural and commercial center. The impact was so huge that he became a one man metropolitan entrepreneur. He was so busy with his real estate holdings, the Los Angeles Railway, and industrial development of Southern California, that he was delayed in his involvement of building beyond Covina. Pacific Electric lines were spreading all over Southern California like spider webs. It was not until August 30, 1909 that the *Pomona Progress* reported that PE surveyors were checking on a line to San Dimas, and a branch line down to Pomona. Actually the PE was first interested in the rock and gravel quarry business in Sycamore Canyon, above San Dimas.

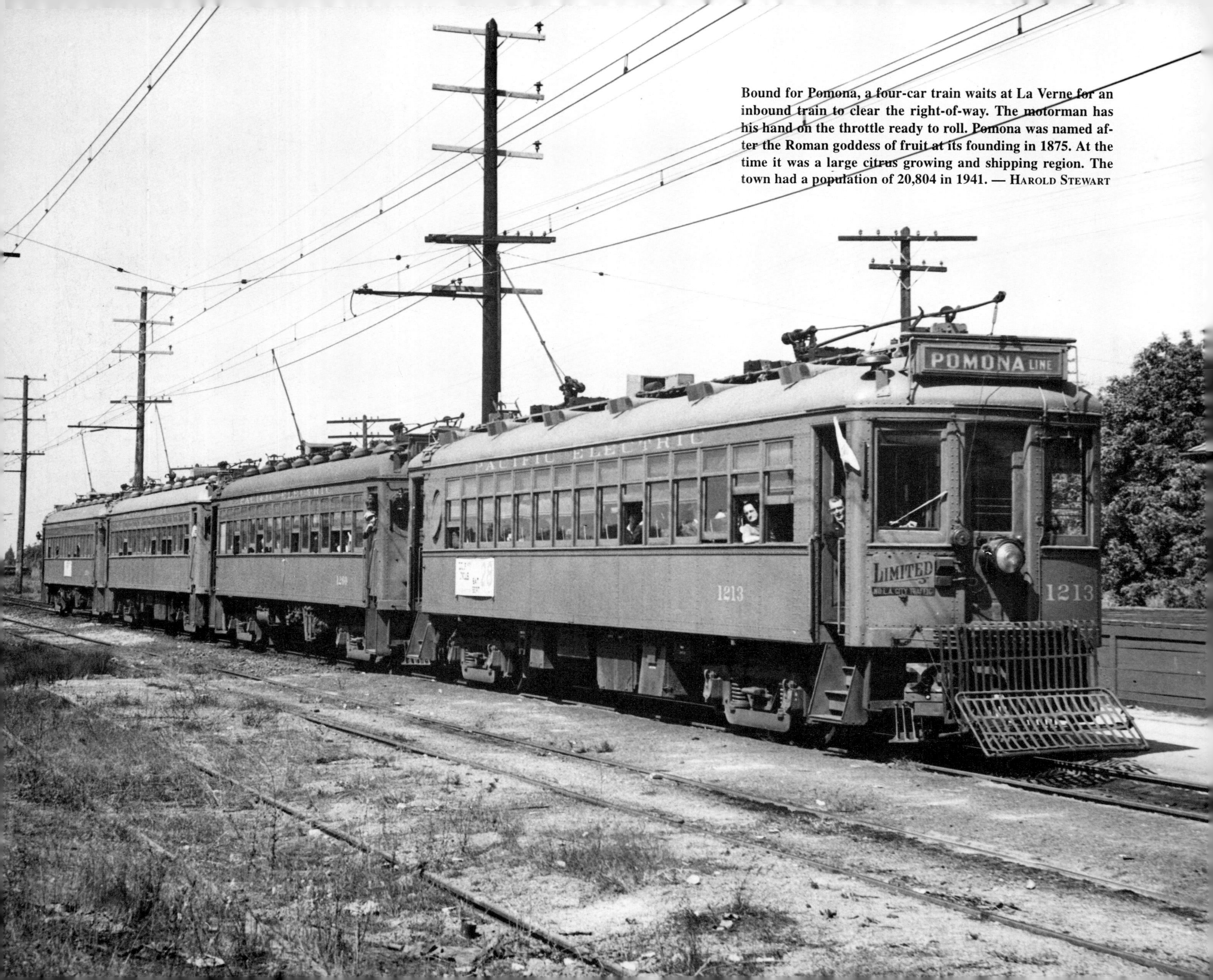

Bound for Pomona, a four-car train waits at La Verne for an inbound train to clear the right-of-way. The motorman has his hand on the throttle ready to roll. Pomona was named after the Roman goddess of fruit at its founding in 1875. At the time it was a large citrus growing and shipping region. The town had a population of 20,804 in 1941. — Harold Stewart

No. 1203 rolls down the main line toward La Verne as it approaches the branch to downtown Pomona. The single car train will wait at La Verne for an inbound meet. — CHARLES D. SAVAGE

Los Angeles bound train No. 36 rolls north along Garey Avenue in the northern part of Pomona. The car has just cleared Pearl Street. — BILL EVERETT COLLECTION

No. 1253 as part of a two-car train, rolls along the Palm tree lined Garey Avenue of North Pomona. Soon it will cross the Southern Pacific and Union Pacific main lines in downtown Pomona. — IVAN BAKER - CRAIG RASMUSSEN COLLECTION

The *Pomona Progress* reported in January 1910 that Pacific Electric chief engineer George Pillsbury was conferring with citizens of San Dimas and Pomona about extending the line beyond Covina through San Dimas, and Lordsburg (present day La Verne), with a connection to Pomona at North Pomona. Actual work on the extension got underway on July 24, 1910, where a large grading camp was established on the Cheney Ranch between San Dimas and Charter Oak. The extension would be 6.27 miles of single track, 1.02 miles of spur, and 0.12 miles of double track, making a distance of 7.53 miles. Also the railroad to the rock and gravel quarry in Sycamore Canyon, north of San Dimas, got underway on August 6, 1910. A huge amount of earth had to be moved to provide a right-of-way along the precipitous side of the canyon.

Two steam shovels began the grading around Lone Hill. On October 23, 1910, a crew working from Covina and

The tower man in the overhead signal box has lowered the crossing gates protecting the Southern Pacific and Union Pacific main lines in Pomona. Southern Pacific steam locomotive No. 1736, which has been switching in the Pomona area, has rights over all traffic. An outbound Pacific Electric car waits patiently for the crossing gates to lift. Southern Pacific's Pomona Station is off to the left. — Harold Stewart

With the Union Pacific and Southern Pacific tracks clear, Los Angeles bound cars Nos. 1375 and 1213 clatter across the diamonds along Garey Avenue. Union Pacific's Pomona station may be seen off to the right. — Harold Stewart

the crew working west from San Dimas, met at Charter Oak with a spike driving ceremony. All through November the rails were bonded, poles erected, the overhead constructed. The route was groomed for the start of service. The citizens of Pomona kept after Huntington to extend service to their community, then they were shocked to learn that on November 1, 1910, that Huntington was bowing out of his interest in the Pacific Electric, and had sold his 50 percent to the Southern Pacific. Although sharing ownership with the Southern Pacific had worked out well, and the SP was willing to spend millions on expansion of the system, the SP was capable of stomping out the wishes of Henry E. Huntington. Obvious the SP was more after the rock and gravel trade than extending to Pomona.

Passenger service to San Dimas began on March 1, 1911. It was a single track line to Covina, then double track from Covina to Los Angeles. There remained a seven mile gap between San Dimas and Pomona. With the Southern Pacific now in 100 percent control it became obvious it would be thrifty to electrify the SP line from San Dimas into Pomona. The *Pomona Progress* reported August 23, 1911: "Rumors have it that the Pacific Electric is about to begin work of connecting the Pomona trolley system with the Covina Branch and that this may possibly be done by the first of the next year." Paul Shoup, born in San Bernardino, rose through the ranks of the Southern Pacific, became president of the Pacific Electric following Huntington.

Shoup stated on May 22, 1912, that the PE planned to electrify the single track SP line into Pomona and Los Angeles service should start shortly. Gangs were involved in overhead wire installation, and a connection was made with the Claremont power station of the Pacific Light & Power Company for current. Service into Pomona began August 31, 1912 with a train to Los Angeles every hour. Connections to Claremont and Upland, over rails of the Ontario & San Antonio Heights Railway, were afforded from Pomona Junction, a half mile north of Pomona. Los Angeles passengers had to wait at the North Pomona Junction for service into Los Angeles. Until a direct line was built in 1914 between LaVerne and North Pomona, direct service to Upland did not begin until July 11, 1914.

The Pomona Yard, just off Garey Street at East Fourth Avenue, was the storage yard for Pomona's "Big Red Cars." — Harold Stewart

Pacific Electric car No. 1213 rolls off Garey Avenue onto East Fifth Avenue bound for the PE station, circa 1941. — Bill Everett Collection

Two San Bernardino 1200-class interurban cars, Nos. 1214 and 1212, roll along the San Bernardino Line near La Verne. La Verne was another citrus-growing and packing center. La Verne originated as Lordsburg during the 1890 land boom. When the real estate bubble burst the town dwindled. In 1916, the town changed its name to La Verne. Pacific Electric cars Nos. 1200 to 1221 were known as the San Bernardino 1200's. Each car was complete with a toilet in each end of the car, and seated 60 passengers.— Donald Duke Collection

Los Angeles County Fair Specials

With abandonment of all tracks beyond Ganesha Junction, many cars were stored on each and every siding. In this view, cars Nos. 1201, 1249, 1257, 1244, 1238 and 1241 are stored on Badillo Street, east of Citrus Street, in Covina. Circa 1948. — Craig Rasmussen Collection

Although regular passenger service was discontinued to Pomona in 1941, special trains continued to service the Los Angeles County Fair in North Pomona. The fair grounds, located just north of Ganesha Park, were open during the last two weeks of September. The fair, started in 1922 on a 175-acre site. It was known as the "biggest county fair in America." A million visitors flocked to see livestock, domestic arts, home cooking, canning and dairy products. In the scene above, No. 1242 leads a fair special through El Monte. — Andy Payne

Owl Eyed interurban car No. 1252 leads a three-car Los Angeles County Fair special west of La Verne. All special trains carried white flags, indicating a "extra." The flag may be seen at the right of the car front. The fair was discontinued during the World War II years. — Charles D. Savage

Two special trains unload their passengers at the Los Angeles County Fair station. When unloading was completed, the trains pulled on down to Ganesha Junction, reversed ends, and were ready for the return run. — Bill Everett Collection

A 1941 edition of the Los Angeles County Fair special carries a Pomona Line destination sign as all the metal signs which hung in front were taken or were being used. The scene is at La Verne waiting for trackage rights. — Donald Duke Collection

A three-car train loads fair passengers at the Los Angeles County Fair station. The date is September 25, 1949. — Andy Payne

PACIFIC ELECTRIC RAILWAY TIME TABLE

SERVICE LEAVING
Los Angeles County Fair Grounds

Leave Fair Grounds for Los Angeles	Leave Fair Grounds for San Bernardino	Leave Fair Grounds for Pomona
† 6.24am	S-B 8.05am	†T 7.05am
S 6.34	†-B 8.10	S-T 7.09
† 6.44	B10.05	T 9.19
† 7.44	B12.05pm	10.19
S 7.45	B 2.05	T11.19
S-B 8.05	B 4.05	12.19pm
†-B 8.10	B 5.25	T 1.19
9.47	S-B 8.48	2.19
B10.05	†-B 8.57	T 3.19
11.47	‡-A10.53	4.19
B12.05am	SS-A11.17	S 5.19
1.47		† 5.22
2.47		5.38
3.47		‡-T 6.10
4.47		Sat-T6.17
S 5.47		S-T 6.19
† 5.55		† 7.01
6.39		S 7.29
7.37		† 7.31
8.27		T10.27
9.17		
10.07		
10.53		
SS11.17		

ALL PACIFIC ELECTRIC SERVICE DEPARTS FROM NORTH ENTRANCE

†—Daily except Sunday.
‡—Daily except Saturday and Sunday.
S—Sunday only.
Sat—Saturday only.
SS—Saturday and Sunday only.
A—Los Angeles Train—connection at La Verne for points east.
B—Motor Coach from Fair Grounds—connections at La Verne.
T—Connection at Pomona Junction for Claremont.

In effect Sept. 15th to Oct. 1st, Inclusive, 1939

H. O. MARLER
Passenger Traffic Manager
Pacific Electric Bldg., Los Angeles, Cal.

Form 8B 20M—9-6-39
(See other side for Motor Transit Service)

Pomona Local Lines

The thriving city of Pomona was founded in 1875, and grew to some size during the land boom of the 1880's in Southern California. East of Covina, it was the only town which had a considerable population except for Riverside and San Bernardino. Near the turn of the century, it had five different systems of public transportation. Three were slow moving horse car lines, and the other two were steam dummy lines.

The Southern Pacific obtained one of the steam dummy lines in 1907, thus giving Henry E. Huntington a wedge or possibly an entry for his Pacific Electric. All five of the systems were modest in size and certainly over rickety track. Since Huntington spent a lot of time in New York, the application for a local franchise was not fulfilled. No trackage had been built, nor had he taken over any of the operating lines. He forfeited his franchise fee which was considerable at the time.

On his return to Southern California, the Pacific Electric once again applied for local service in Pomona, and nearly defaulted once again because of the lack of construction. The franchise required that some effort would be made to build a line or lines. Crews were sent to Pomona to grade and lay some track while the Pomona extension of the interurban line to Pomona took a back seat. The franchise was saved.

When the Pacific Electric had completed three single-track routes in Pomona, which aggregated some 10.43 miles of track, it was divided into 1.24 miles of double or passing track, 7.89 miles of single track, and .006 miles of track into a storage area.

A entirely new substation was built at 1st and Garey Avenue to provide the 600 volt direct-current power to run the cars. A two block-long yard was built at 5th & Garey, and a local and interurban station was proposed on Garey. It never came to pass. The three Pacific Electric local line routes were:

Riverside & Arlington No. 10 called the *Alfarata*, came over to the Pomona Local Lines when Henry Huntington took over the line. It ran in Pomona for several years. This car participated in the San Bernardino welcome of the through line between Los Angeles and San Bernardino on July 11, 1914. — Donald Duke Collection

Garey & Park Avenue Line - This line started in the south of Pomona, ran up Garey Avenue to Holt Avenue while passing the Pomona Valley Cemetery, then west to Ganesha Park in the northwest part of Pomona. Service was every 15 minutes.

West Second Street & Park Avenue Line - Started in the west part of Pomona, where the industries were located, ran east to Garey Avenue, then duplicated the route of the above line to Ganesha Park. Part of the line ran on the interurban route from La Verne to central Pomona. Cars ran about every half hour.

Holt & East Fifth Street Line - This line started in the east end of Pomona, at the Los Angeles/San Bernardino County Line and ran west on Fifth, through the downtown district to Garey, then north on Garey to Holt, then west on Holt to Garfield Park. Cars ran every 40 minutes.

All lines crossed the Union Pacific and Southern Pacific main lines on the north part of Pomona, and passed the respective road depots. Service was started with cars with an open section on each end of the car, and a closed section in the middle. As patronage began to wane, birney cars came on the scene in 1918, to be followed by city cars that were center entrance cars or which buffs called "Dragon Cars," because the ends were higher than the middle. Application to abandon all service was applied for in early 1924, and granted October 1, 1924. The "Dragon Cars" were shipped to the Pasadena Local Lines.

Pacific Electric center-entrance cars, often called *Dragon Cars* because of their appearance, and were used in local service in Pomona. On abandonment of service they were moved to Pasadena Local Lines. In New York, cars of this type were called *Battleships*. — Donald Duke Collection

Single-truck closed cars, just like No. 47, were used daily and also in owl service in Pomona for years. — Donald Duke Collection

The 170-class city-suburban cars were capable of operating on either 600 or 1200 volts. Quite unique for the time. These cars were used mostly on the Pomona-Claremont-Ontario Line which used both for voltages of overhead power. The 170-class cars were built for the Southern Pacific for use in the San Francisco Bay area, but did not work out well and were sold to the Pacific Electric in 1913. — Donald Duke Collection

Upland to Pomona

In the meantime, Henry E. Huntington and William G. Kerckhoff, the two principals in the Pacific Light & Power Company, purchased the electric power system of the Ontario Electric Company, and its subsidiary the Ontario & San Antonio Heights Railroad Company. The purchase was consummated during April 1902.

The Ontario & San Antonio Heights Railroad Company began as a mule car line in 1887, running up the great hill from Ontario to the mountain community of San Antonio Heights, a distance of 8.5 miles. Its rails started in Ontario at the Southern Pacific station, and ran in the median of Euclid Avenue, by way of Upland to San Antonio Heights the location of the Ontario Electric Company's power plant. The mule hauled the car up the hill, then stepped on a platform and had a free ride back to Ontario. The line was electrified in 1895. The *Pomona Progress* reported in its January 16, 1906 issue, that a citizens committee from Upland, Claremont, North Pomona, and San Dimas were pushing the Ontario & San Antonio Heights Railroad to extend their line from Upland into Pomona. Kerckhoff fronting for the Pacific Light & Power Company surveyed the proposed route and thought the line would be good for the company. Huntington did not wish to involve his Pacific Electric system in the project for some unknown reason. An abortive start was made in late 1907, and it was late 1911 before rails were extended from Upland to Claremont. By mid-December 1911 the line into Pomona was completed except for the stringing of the overhead trolley wire.

Kerckhoff's Ontario & San Antonio Heights Railroad opened its interurban extension from Claremont into Pomona on January 1, 1912, temporarily relegating the line to Los Angeles to secondary status by Pomonans. A great celebration welcoming the Kerckhoff line was held on January 7th to a huge throng in Pomona. In the meantime, the PE line extended to San Dimas and they promised the PE would be in Pomona in late January. With the seven mile extension over SP tracks being groomed, it would be August 31, 1912 before cars were run between Pomona and Los Angeles.

The Pacific Electric purchased the Ontario & San Antonio Heights Railroad Company as a result of the 1911 "Great Merger' with its 16 miles of track on April 1, 1912. The line was built with a single track between Upland and Pomona. Paul Shoup, who became president of the Pacific Electric, following Henry Huntington, stated that a connection would be made between La Verne and North Pomona in order to provide through service between Los Angeles and Upland.

This view shows the San Antonio Park Station of the Ontario & San Antonio Heights Railroad which Henry E. Huntington had a vested interest. The scene shows the station in 1909, which was built as a passenger transfer facility between the railroad and auto stages to Camp Baldy. The station was of the omnipresent rock and boulders which were free every place on the ground just for the picking.

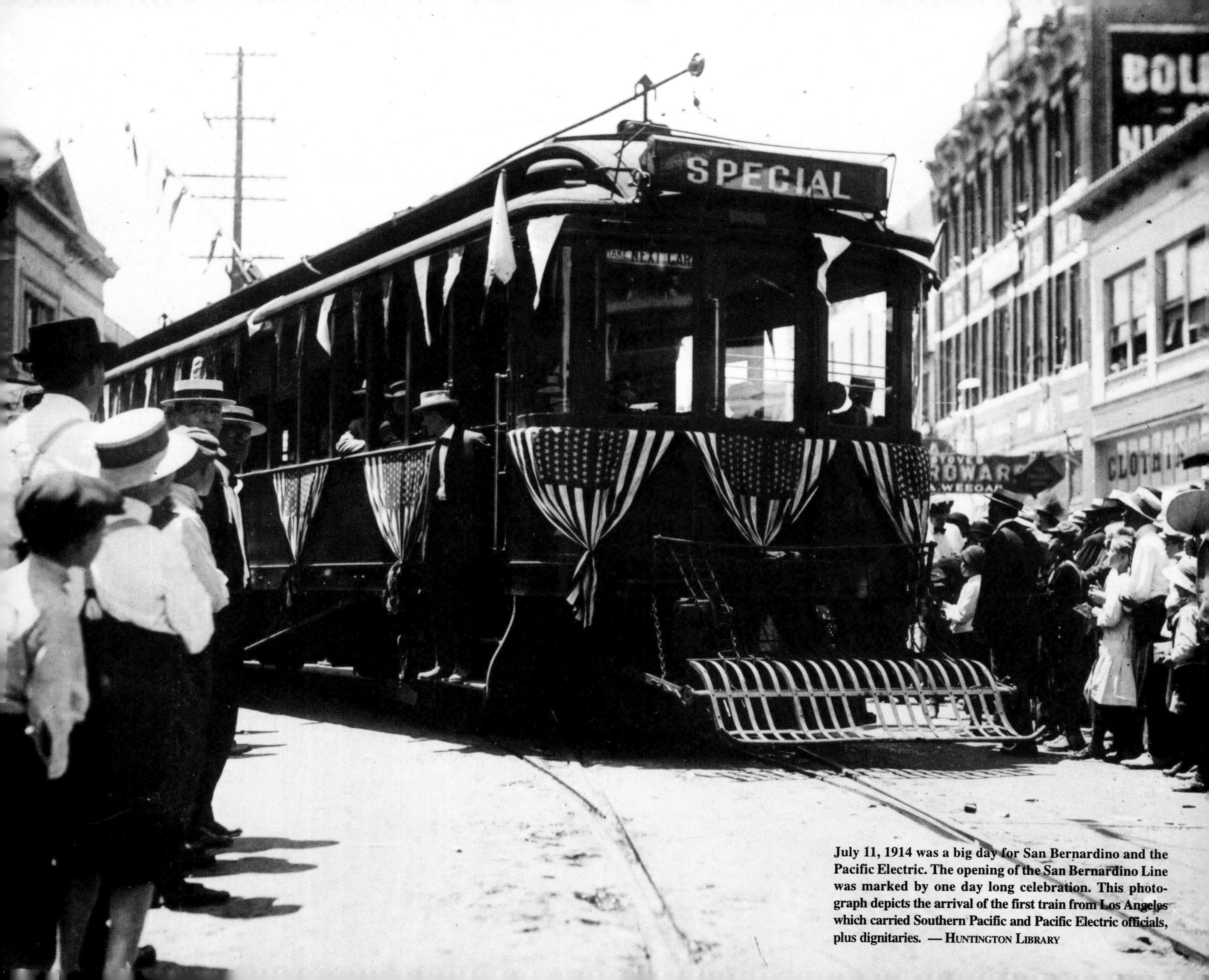

July 11, 1914 was a big day for San Bernardino and the Pacific Electric. The opening of the San Bernardino Line was marked by one day long celebration. This photograph depicts the arrival of the first train from Los Angeles which carried Southern Pacific and Pacific Electric officials, plus dignitaries. — HUNTINGTON LIBRARY

San Bernardino Line

Construction was now taken up to close the 21.63 mile gap between Upland and San Bernardino. With Henry Huntington out of the picture, and Southern Pacific in full control of the Pacific Electric, it was projected that the line would be completed sometime in 1914. It was estimated that the cost of construction would run some $1,424,000. On May 28, 1913 it was announced that the contract for completing the line had been awarded to Grant Brothers, Southern Pacific's railroad contractor. Grant Brothers had rebuilt S.P. lines in Arizona and rebuilt the entire El Paso & Southwestern Railway, recently acquired by the Southern Pacific from Phelps Dodge Corporation.

Grant Brothers began construction on both ends of the line at the same time, working toward the middle. With modern steam shovels to make cuts and fills, and the latest type graders, it was estimated the line would be completed in a year's time. There was a great deal of bridge and fill work on the San Bernardino end of the line, raising the line up and over the Santa Fe tracks and yards. Working east from Upland, Etiwanda was reached January 20, 1914. The whole extension was built to first-class standards, with rock ballast, 120 lb. rails, and heavy overhead.

The *Los Angeles Times* stated on April 9, 1914, that it was expected that electric cars would be running between Los Angeles and San Bernardino sometime in May. That construction work was moving at a rapid pace, and the rails and overhead were in except for the bridge over Lytle Creek wash. Lytle Creek could be a bear during the rainy season as water would come thundering down the canyons and landing in the wash. The dry wash could become a thundering river, washing out everything in its path. So great care was made to protect the right-of-way at this point.

D. W. Pontius, passenger traffic manager for the Pacific Electric announced on June 3, 1914; "It will be July 1st before we can get regular service inaugurated to Los Angeles from San Bernardino. There is still some finishing work to be done."

The formal opening of the new San Bernardino Line was held on July 12, 1914. The line extended 59 miles from downtown Los Angeles to the center of San Bernardino. It was the longest line on the PE system, and it represented an expenditure of $1,424,000. A lot of bucks for the time. The new line penetrated the heart of the citrus belt, and ran through some fertile farm land, which was destined to bring in lots of freight revenue. The San Bernardino Line increased the system trackage to 1,067 miles.

The area covered was not heavily populated beyond Pomona at the time. The line traversed much undeveloped areas beyond the orange groves, and there were long stretches where there were no towns of any great importance. Hence the running time over the line could be operated at high-speed.

Construction was first-class. All bridges on the line were built of concrete-arch construction, with provision for double track should it become necessary to install another line. Operation in city streets was found only in high density areas, otherwise the entire line was on private right-of-way.

The opening of the San Bernardino Line was marked by one huge celebration in San Bernardino, lasting the whole day, and into the night. Upon the arrival of the first train from Los Angeles, carrying dignitaries from all along the line, as well as Pacific Electric and Southern Pacific officials, the three-car train pulled up to the Pacific Electric station. The first train was covered with red, white, and blue bunting from the pilot to the marker lights. Some 20,000 people were on hand to welcome this train.

After the dignitaries left their train, Paul Shoup, president of the Pacific Electric gave a short talk. He ended his message with, "On behalf of the officers and stockholders of the railroad, I dedicate this day as Pacific Electric day, and acknowledge in deep appreciation of the partnership between the cities along the new line." It was now time for the spike driving. P. A. Dessens, mayor of Alta Loma stepped up and said, "Alta Loma presents this silver spike with the hope that it will prove to be taken of a new solidarity of interest throughout the orange land." The spike was driven first by Mayor H. H. Rose of Los Angeles, and followed by Acting Mayor Claude R. Davidson of San Bernardino. The spike was driven into an orangewood tie presented by the San Bernardino Chamber of Commerce.

Following the speeches, mayors of on-line towns had a word to say. This was followed by a pageant staged by the famous John S. McGroarty, author of the well-known Mission Play. McGroarty was also the correspondent from the *Los Angeles Times*.

As noon approached, a street parade was held which led to Lugo Park. Here, additional speeches were given, followed by a band concert while spectators ate their picnic lunch. In mid-afternoon a baseball game was held between Riverside and San Bernardino county officials. In the evening the dignitaries adjourned to the Contadores Club, where a formal dinner was held. Just 20 years earlier, Paul Shoup began his railroad career at San Bernardino as a ticket seller at the San Bernardino Motor Road depot.

With operations under way, the Pacific Electric began operating at 1,200 volts from Covina Junction (later to be called Valley Junction) all the way to San Bernardino. All substations between Covina Junction to Upland switched over from 600 volts of power when the complete line opened. Under the 600 volt system, substations were located five miles apart. Substation under the 1,200 volt system were placed ten miles apart. The 1,200 volt substations were located at Ramona Park (Alhambra), Vineland (Baldwin Park), North Pomona, Etiwanda, and San Bernardino.

Each substation was equipped with a 15,000 volt three-phase motor directly connected to a 1,200 volt direct current generator. The four motors could be used in parallel on a 600 volt car, and two motors were in series for the 1,200 volt car. When a train approached the 1,200 volt section, the car would pull up and the motorman would throw the switch to 1,200 volts. For the 1000-series cars the motorman had to get down on the ground and throw a switch under the car for 1,200 volts. On the 1200 and 1300-class cars a switch was thrown alongside the controller. A 600 volt car could not operate on the 1,200 volts section, otherwise the car would burn out its motors. A car or locomotive with the switch set at 1,200 volts could operate on 600 volts, but not effectively. So at Covina Junction they had to reverse the switch on Los Angeles bound trains.

A word about the two 1000-class cars which made the first run. Following the "Great Merger" of 1911 under Southern Pacific control, the Pacific Electric became one traction empire that would ultimately cover over 1,067 miles of track and represent more than ten percent of the United States interurban investment.

The PE already had a sizeable fleet of fast wooden interurban cars from all the predecessor and merged companies, but with the expansions planned the PE would need an infusion of new rolling stock. A new order for the 1000-class cars was placed out for bid. These cars would be larger and more powerful than anything on the roster.

In anticipation of the new San Bernardino Line, planned as a 1,200 volt line, the 1000-class cars would be equipped for either 600 or 1,200 volt D.C. power supply. Although the class would be of wood construction, the 1000-class would be built on an all-steel underframe. The design would be utilitarian, with nearly flat ends, with curved glass corners. Each car was to be arranged for double-end, multiple-unit operation with a vestibule and steps at the ends of the cars.

The Jewett Car Company of Newark, Ohio, won the bid for the first 45 cars. Interiors were divided into a closed and open section. Each car would have a roof roll destination sign, air whistle, a gong, and moveable arc headlight. A trolley pole for power was mounted on each end of the roof.

The crowd of thousands went wild when the first train arrived. The cars were festooned with banners and bunting. There were speeches, presentation, and a spike driving. Afterward a picnic and bank concert were held in the park. — Huntington Library

Shortly after opening of the line, a single car, bound for Los Angeles, was photographed at Alta Loma. The station was located on Amethyst Street. — Donald Duke Collection

When the Southern Pacific took over the direction of the Pacific Electric, as a result of the Great Merger, in order to impress the public they purchased many new cars. Among them was the 1000-class cars which could operate on 600 or 1200 volts. These slick cars were fast and had a quick pickup. Crews called them "jackrabbits." (LEFT) The typical front end of a 1000-class car. (ABOVE) No. 1036 out on the San Bernardino Line. There are no passengers aboard because the car was being used as a training car this day, a few miles west of San Bernardino. — DONALD DUKE COLLECTION

The first cars arrived in 1913 without air brakes and electrical equipment which were to be installed by the PE shops. High-speed Brill M.C.B. trucks came with each car. Traction motors, multiple-unit control, and air brakes were supplied to the PE by Westinghouse. Once installed the 1000-class cars were first used on the Long Beach, San Pedro, Pomona, and Northern Division lines.

With the switch over from 600 to 1,200 volts on July 11, 1914, the 1000-class cars which opened the line ran on 600 volts to Covina Junction and 1,200 volts to San Bernardino. The tenure of the 1000-class on the San Bernardino Line came to a halt with the coming of the all-steel 1200-class cars. However the 1000-class were used in rush hour service to El Monte until 1940. The No. 1036 made the last scheduled run on November 1, 1941.

Since the line was 59 miles in length, 14 1000-class cars were equipped with lavatory accommodations. These were cars Nos. 1030-1038, and Nos. 1040-1044. Once the 1200-class cars arrived, the water tanks and toilets were removed, and the open section enclosed.

According to a conversation with O. A. Smith, president of the Pacific Electric, he stated that it was planned to convert the heavily traveled interurban lines to 1,200 volts to speed operations and to cut down on the number of substations. The idea never bore fruit. All of the new steel electric locomotives were also equipped for 600 and 1,200 volt operation.

Now that the San Bernardino Line was completed, the Pacific Electric had access to affiliated San Bernardino Valley Traction Company a former Huntington owned property. This included lines to Arrowhead, Highland, Colton, Patton, and Redlands. It was now time to connect San Bernardino with Riverside, and the former lines of the Riverside & Arlington Railway.

Through passenger service began immediately between Los Angeles and San Bernardino with ten round trips daily. Two trains were "limited" trains. Train No. 34 to Los Angeles was called the *Angel City Limited.* It left San Bernardino at 7:45 A.M. and arrived in Los Angeles at 9:30 A.M. The *Citrus Belt Limited*, train No. 77, left Los Angeles at 4:35 P.M. and arrived in San Bernardino at 6:58 P.M. Running time was one hour and 45 minutes. All other trains

A two-car set of box motors meets No. 1362, in the yards behind the San Bernardino station. The box motors are bound for Los Angeles, and No. 1362 is working as a franchise car. — JACK WHITMEYER

The front side of the San Bernardino Pacific Electric/Southern Pacific station. It was located at 549 Third Street. All trains entered the station from the rear. — DONALD DUKE COLLECTION

Pacific Electric No. 1036 waits for its run to Los Angeles, while resting alongside the San Bernardino carbarn. — DONALD DUKE COLLECTION

made a stop on flag and made the 59 mile run in approximately two hours and five minutes.

There were 30 trains daily between Los Angeles and Covina, and 14 trains to Pomona (via Covina) daily. Both towns were within the Los Angeles area commute district.

With the completion of the line to Riverside which was finished March 21, 1914, generally the train to Riverside was cut off the back end of the San Bernardino train at Riverside Junction (Rialto). This junction in timetables was called Rialto Junction, and in early employee timetables it was called Riverside Junction.

There were two major bottlenecks on the line when first opened. The first was that all trains had to dip down into Pomona, which required seven miles of unnecessary travel. The Lordsburg (San Dimas) cutoff between La Verne and North Pomona was completed on November 4, 1914. It was just one and one-half miles long and saved 20 minutes running time. Why it was not built in the first place remains a mystery!

The other bottleneck was between Covina and La Verne which was the trackage over the Southern Pacific. Since the line was not equipped with signals, the single track was protected by a staff system. The staff machines were located at Barranca Street (Covina), Lone Hill, San Dimas, La Verne and North Pomona. Every train passing through each section was required to stop at each machine. If there was a train coming in the opposite direction the staff would not set up. At the end of each section the conductor had to release the section traveled over and set the staff ahead. To set the machine took only about 60 seconds, but was a constant irritation to passengers. Since nearly 50 trains per day traveled this section, it only seems ridiculous that they did not signal it? The line was double-track to Covina, protected by staff system to North Pomona, then operated by employee timetable and train orders from the dispatcher in Los Angeles. Telephones were set up along the line, and the conductor would have to call in and then write out a train order.

The *Los Angeles Times* reported an interesting occur-

A look at the well manicured right-of-way of the San Bernardino Line. I believe this is at the Masonic Home stop, just east of Covina, in the middle of the vast orange groves which were located all along the line. Citrus provided the Pacific Electric with many refrigerator loads of freight. — Donald Duke Collection

Pacific Electric's new 1200-class cars were the "creme-de-la-creme" of interurban equipment.These all-steel high-speed electric cars incorporated all the latest developments of the time. Designed for both 600 and 1200 volt operation, cars Nos. 1200 through 1221 were also equipped with toilets at both ends of the cars. This scene was taken at PE's 7th and Central Shops. — Donald Duke Collection

rence that happened on the San Bernardino Line at Lone Hill on June 4, 1915. An inbound train from Pomona pulled up to the staff system at Lone Hill stop at 11:05 P.M., and conductor Jack Flake stepped down to set the staff machine, and to release the one just traveled on. Two armed masked bandits came out of the trees and held up Flake. One bandit entered the car and made all the passengers, including motorman H. D. Parker get off, line up with hands raised. They took all wallets, purses, watches, and anything of value. From Flake they took $200 from his case, a whole days collections. Then they made them all get on the car, while they escaped in the dark. The robbery was reported to the police at Covina, but the bandits were long gone.

The handling of freight on the San Bernardino Line began immediately after its opening. Down through the years it became one of the most lucrative sources of income as passenger traffic began to fall off. The San Bernardino Line was among PE's big three as far as freight was concerned. First was Los Angeles-Long Beach Harbor, second was El Segundo, and third was the San Bernardino Line. The handling of sack mail and express by the use of box motors was heavier on the line than any other on the system.

With all the planned expansion, the Pacific Electric decided to build up its fleet of long distance interurban cars. The PE was well satisfied with its 1000-class cars and was preparing for another fleet of wooden equipment. Then came the tragic Vineyard wreck on July 11, 1913. Two sets of wooden cars ran into each other in the fog at Vineyard on the Western Division. Twelve passengers were killed and more than 200 others injured. It was decided the new fleet would have all-steel bodies. Thus was born the 1200-class interurban car.

A three-car train of 1200-class cars speeds toward La Verne passing through the Empire of the Orange. La Verne was less than half-way along the San Bernardino Line. — CHARLES D. SAVAGE

San Dimas

No. 1200 is on an eastbound run at San Dimas, circa September 1940.The motorman has his hand on the controller, ready to start the car as soon as he receives the "go-ahead" signal from the conductor. (LEFT) Owl Eyed No. 1373 works through the vinyards near Etiwanda in 1938. — Both Donald Duke Collection

A San Bernardino Line express pulls into the passing siding at Berkeley Avenue, waiting for a westbound to roll by, and clear the line. — Donald Duke Collection (LEFT) No. 1372 meets a Pacific Electric local bus at San Dimas in 1939. — Ivan Baker - Craig Rasmussen Collection

After leaving the San Bernardino station, bound for Los Angeles, No. 1211 rolls along Rialto Avenue in San Bernardino. There were several blocks of street running before the private right-of-way began. — CHARLES D. SAVAGE

An order was placed with the Pressed Steel Car Co. of Pittsburg, Pennsylvania, early in 1914 for 24 steel interurban cars which could operate on either 600 or 1,200 volts. Twenty-two of the cars would be standard coaches, and two were to be combination of baggage-coach design. Car bodies were to be framed in sheet steel, with a heavy steel underframe. High-speed, seven-foot wheelbase trucks were to be employed, and each car was to be equipped with four 150 hp. General Electric traction motors geared for 70 m.p.h. maximum speed. Each car was to be divided with one third smoking section and two thirds non-smoking. On arrival the coaches were assigned Nos. 1200-1221, and the combines were numbered Nos. 1370-1371. A lavatory was to be provided in each end of each coach and on one end of the combines. The cars were an immediate success.

Six years later, in 1921, the Pacific Electric ordered another 30 identical cars for its Southern Division lines to Long Beach, San Pedro, and Santa Ana except these cars lacked the toilets. Twenty were equipped with motors, while ten were non-motor cars, known as trailer cars. They had operating controls, but lacked motors or trolley poles. As long as traffic remained strong the cars were used continuously. When patronage dropped off during the depression, the trailers were seen less and less. During World War II they were pressed into service.

With the increase in land use and the building of towns all along the San Bernardino Line during the 1920 period, passengers were swinging to the automobile for transpor-

The station in San Bernardino appears to be empty, as it is between trains. No. 1258 patiently waits for the next run to Los Angeles. — CHARLES D. SAVAGE

A huge steamer trunk and a lot of packages, and express, are being unloaded from the front end of No. 1371 as the train paused at Claremont in 1935. — CHARLES D. SAVAGE

No. 1209, bound for San Bernardino, clatters across a wood trestle on a high fill as the interurban approaches Bench stop. — CHARLES D. SAVAGE

Ralph Melching aboard a Railroad Booster special train at La Verne, snapped this photograph as car No. 1211 heads for Los Angeles. Melching was aboard No. 1000, and the date was September 11, 1938, just two years after the Railroad Boosters was formed.

tation. Where trains consisted of several cars, they slowly were cut to one through car to San Bernardino and a cut-off car to Riverside. On July 20, 1936 interurban service to Redlands was discontinued, and on June 9, 1940 all though service was cut to Riverside. On that same day there were only four trains running between Los Angeles and San Bernardino. On November 1, 1941 all interurban service ended to Pomona. On that same date all service ended beyond Baldwin Park, except for two morning and evening rush hour commuter trains to Covina. On March 28, 1947 service to Covina ended with all trains tying up at Baldwin Park. On October 15, 1950 service ended between Los Angeles and Baldwin Park.

While passenger service was discontinued due to the greater swing to automobiles, freight service between Los Angeles to San Bernardino was booming. The PE was handling more sack mail and Railway Express. (See the section on freight).

On a hot day in 1939, the motorman has his door open to catch a breeze as his No. 1221 races for San Bernardino. This steel viaduct is over the Santa Fe yard tracks in San Bernardino. — Charles D. Savage

There were several concrete arch bridges on the San Bernardino Line. In this view, No. 1207 dashes across Lytle Creek just west of San Bernardino. Lytle Creek is dry at this time, but when it rains in the mountains the creek becomes a raging river of water. — CHARLES D. SAVAGE

During 1938 and 1939, a major rebuilding program was taken by the Pacific Electric to upgrade and modernize its equipment. Cars No. 1216-1221 underwent this streamlining. Patterned after Southern Pacific's *Daylight* streamliners, the cars were provided with tubular frame revolving seats, bullseye lighting, electric marker lights, faired-in-the-roof destination signs, and a striking red and orange coat of paint. Flashy speed wings appeared on the sides and front ends of the cars. All work was accomplished at the Pacific Electric Torrance Shops. — DONALD DUKE COLLECTION

Modernized No. 1217 waits in 1941 at the San Bernardino station for a run into Los Angeles. The Motor Transit bus, a PE subsidiary, ran into the mountain country. — CHARLES D. SAVAGE

A Los Angeles Limited pulls up to the San Dimas station. Butterfly cars Nos. 1220-1219, are on train No. 130. The official train numbers were hung in the left hand front window. — Harold Stewart

The agent was watering the station lawn, while No. 1217 pulls up to the station. No. 1217 is bound for Los Angeles. — Bill Everett Collection (LEFT) No. 1218 takes off for Los Angeles after making a quick stop at the Upland station. — Donald Duke Collection

No. 1212 rolls along Rialto Avenue, bound for the San Bernardino station. The semaphore signal was protection for Santa Fe Railway's Redland Loop Line. You will note there was little highway traffic on the street in 1939. — CHARLES D. SAVAGE

An express train rolls through the orange groves of Heyer, just east of Monte Vista. The date is November 1, 1941. Just before World War II began, the use of eclipse fenders on the cars was discontinued. The Los Angeles City Ordinance requiring their use was abolished. — DONALD DUKE COLLECTION

No. 1216, bound for San Bernardino, pulls up to the vine covered Alta Loma station. The agent unloads the latest issue of the *Los Angeles Times* from the motorman's compartment. (LEFT) Butterfly No. 1217 leaves the La Verne station for Los Angeles. Note the PE bus hiding at the end of the station. — BOTH BILL EVERETT COLLECTION

At Rialto, the junction of the San Bernardino and the Riverside lines, trains often met. Here the Riverside car (LEFT) was cut-off the back end of the San Bernardino car (RIGHT). The conductor from the San Bernardino section is in the phone box calling the dispatcher for clearance all the way to San Bernardino. The 1,200 volt powerhouse is in the background to the left. It was 1,200 volts to San Bernardino, but the Riverside Line was only 600 volts. — Harold Stewart

No. 1243 pulls up to the Etiwanda station. George and William Chaffey started the town in 1882. They named the place after an Indian chief in their home state of Michigan. — Donald Duke Collection

The Saint Bernardino Hotel was next to the San Bernardino station. I don't think the customers enjoyed all the noise of trains and talking passengers. It appears to be a flop house. No. 1243 is all loaded and ready to take off for Los Angeles at the appointed time. The motorman is in the center window, awaiting the signal from the conductor. (BELOW) The conductor is on the ground throwing switches into the station. The metal box contained the conductors cash, tickets, transfers and time book. — CHARLES D. SAVAGE.

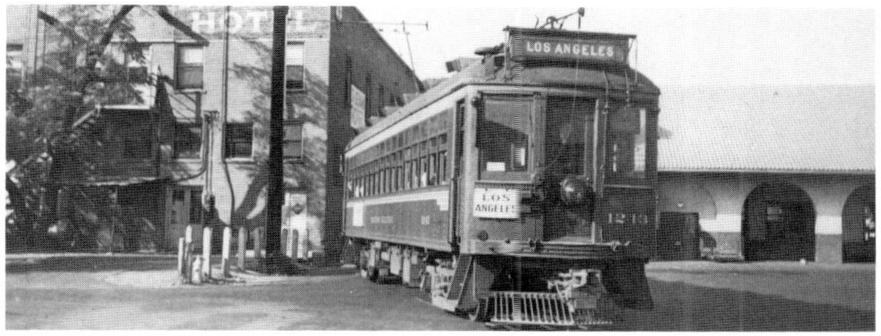

President Oscar Smith's private car, No. 1299, waits at 6th and Main Terminal for its passengers bound for the Orange Show at San Bernardino. The white flag on the left side indicates a special run. — Ralph Melching

A four-car Los Angeles County Fair special train glides down from the elevated terminal at 6th and Main in downtown Los Angeles. The train will head north along San Pedro Street, then to Aliso, and finally onto private right-of-way. — Ralph Melching

A midday train, inbound from Baldwin Park, is bound for the PE terminal. The car is stopped at First and San Pedro street. Note the semaphore traffic signal, a Los Angeles original. — Stuart Liebman

The motorman leans out of his charge to see if his trolley pole is against the wire. When the trolley pole falls, a buzzer sounds and apparently it bounced back onto the trolley wire. — Stephen D. Maguire

A Los Angeles County Fair special has just crossed over the Los Angeles River on the Aliso Street Viaduct, and heads for private right-of-way all the way to Pomona. — RALPH MELCHING

All Northern and Eastern Division rolling stock, in the Los Angeles area, was stored and maintained at the Macy Street shops, carbarn, and yard. — DONALD DUKE COLLECTION

An inbound, to Los Angeles, car from Baldwin Park, rolls along next to Valley Boulevard, then under a rebuilding program. It later became a part of the San Bernardino Freeway. The Macy Street crew quarters is off to the left. — RALPH MELCHING

Valley Junction to El Monte

No. 1220 clatters across the Rio Hondo truss bridge, just a few minutes west of El Monte. (BELOW) No. 1255 rolls along Ramona Boulevard in the southern part of Alhambra. — Both Bill Everett Collection

No. 1253 rolls westbound through the Ramona section of South Alhambra in 1950. The Ramona substation is off to the left out of the picture. — Bill Everett Collection

With the canvas advertising banner loose, and flipping in the wind, as No. 1263 rolls along toward Los Angeles. The train is passing Eastern Avenue, now the site of California State University - Los Angeles. — Ernie Leo (BELOW) An Orange Show special train, on the return to Los Angeles, pulls up to Valley Junction. — Charles D. Savage

El Monte

After leaving Baldwin Park station on April 28, 1950, No. 1212 will make three stops before crossing the dry San Gabriel River. Prior to 1938 the river would become a torrent in the winter. Then several dams, near San Gabriel Canyon, checked its flow. Soon the train will cross the Southern Pacific main line at El Monte. — Andy Payne

Eastbound No. 1203 pulls up to the El Monte station to load and unload passengers. The semaphore protects the Pacific Electric/Southern Pacific crossing just east of the El Monte station. — Donald Duke Collection

Passengers gather at El Monte for the train to Baldwin Park. The El Monte station is off to the left. The semaphore protecting the Southern Pacific main line is at the stop position. Apparently a freight is crossing. — Bill Everett Collection

A midday train is nearly empty after leaving Baldwin Park. It was caught crossing the San Gabriel River, bound for El Monte. The San Gabriel River is nearly dry this time of year, the hot summer. — Donald Duke

The scene is the Baldwin Park station. The "Big Red Car's" replacement can be seen at the right. Drivers are testing the new route. Several more new busses are behind No. 1244. Frankly passenger preferred the trains compared to new busses. — Donald Duke

El Monte to Baldwin Park

No. 1202 pauses at the Baldwin Park station. The train is going nowhere as there is no motorman at the controls. He must be taking a nap inside the car. — DONALD DUKE

The Vineyard substation, located near Baldwin Park, needed a boost of two portable substations during World War II. — BILL EVERETT COLLECTION

This picture looks north along Southern Pacific's Covina Branch at Vineland (Baldwin Park). Note the stop signs on each side of the Pacific Electric track. — IVAN BAKER - CRAIG RASMUSSEN COLLECTION

No. 1226 waits patiently at the end of the line at Baldwin Park, before pulling up to the station, and its run to Los Angeles. — CHARLES D. SAVAGE (LEFT) No 1220 waits for scheduled time at the Baldwin Park station. — BILL EVERETT COLLECTION

Orange Show Specials

The mammoth National Orange Show, was held just south of San Bernardino for a couple of weeks during February each year. When orange was "King" in San Bernardino, it was the prime event of the year. The show presented numerous huge structures made out of citrus. Millions of oranges, lemons, and grapefruit were used in the construction of the displays. For years the Pacific Electric had a display with model trains running around the exhibit. On the left, No. 1260 heads a four-car train bound for the Orange Show. — DONALD DUKE

President of the Pacific Electric, Oscar Smith's special rolls along the San Bernardino Line right-of-way near Alta Loma. The No. 1299 was equipped with a small kitchen to make light meals, and a snack or two. — DONALD DUKE

A three-car train races to the National Orange Show at San Bernardino. It was photographed passing through La Verne. — CHARLES D. SAVAGE

The crew of a National Orange Show special patiently wait for a late inbound meet at San Dimas station. The motorman sits on the eclipse fender, while the conductor of the first car chats with him. The conductor of the last car stares down the track looking for the meet. This scene was photographed in February 1937. — CHARLES D. SAVAGE

An Orange Show special was photographed returning to Los Angeles near San Dimas. One of the original railroad enthusiasts stand on a orange water syphon to take a picture of this special event. — CHARLES D. SAVAGE

In 1939 a Riverside bound train rolls past the Riverside Portland Cement Company plant en route to Riverside. No. 1214 is kicking up some dust as it rolls along a dirt street at Crescent City. — CHARLES D. SAVAGE

Riverside Line

The Riverside Line was a branch off the San Bernardino Line at Rialto, running southeast 9.52 miles to the PE station on Market Street in downtown Riverside. Through service between Los Angeles and Riverside began March 15, 1915. The Riverside Line ran over leased trackage.

In 1907 while the huge Riverside Portland Cement Co. was under construction, just four miles northwest of Riverside, its principal owner William G. Henshaw was attempting to get the Southern Pacific to extend a branch either from Riverside or Bloomington to haul out his products. The Southern Pacific refused. Henshaw then built the Crescent City Railway from the plant to Riverside to a connection with the Santa Fe Railway or the Los Angeles & Salt Lake Railroad. On February 28, 1908, Henshaw convinced the Riverside & Arlington Railway to electrify the line so his employees could reach the plant. A connection was made at Houghton Avenue and Market Street, and trolley service began between Crestmore and Riverside. The Riverside & Arlington was to have all rights over Crescent City Railway steam trains.

The Riverside & Arlington Railway began as an amalgamation of four separate horse car lines running in Riverside. Frank A. Miller electrified the four routes and be-

When trains to San Bernardino and Riverside were in regular operation, midday trains were split at Rialto. During the last months of operation, the Riverside car ran as a shuttle. In this scene, Riverside train No. 1209 is the Riverside-Rialto shuttle. No. 1201 will continue on to Los Angeles. — Harold Stewart

On June 8, 1940, No. 1209 rolls by the Southern Pacific tower at Bloomington, bound for Rialto Junction, and Los Angeles. At Rialto, No. 1209 will attach itself to the rear of the train from San Bernardino. — Donald Duke Collection

A Los Angeles bound single train rolls along Riverside Highway and heads for the tower at Bloomington. Note the heavy automobile traffic! (LEFT) A right-of-way scene on the Riverside Line near Bloomington. The line could stand a weed-burner as it looks more like a branch line rather than the Riverside main line. — Both Harold Stewart

gan electric railway service on April 5, 1899. Although busy, the railway failed to pay off. Miller, a friend of Henry E. Huntington, convinced Huntington to buy the system and connect it to his Pacific Electric Railway. Huntington assumed control in 1903. He announced great plans to connect the Riverside & Arlington Railway with Corona, run down Santa Ana Canyon to connect with his Yorba Linda Line at Stern. He did build to Corona, but that was as far as the trackage went.

Eventually an extension was built to Bloomington, and a connection there with the Southern Pacific, but this four mile line was never electrified by the Riverside & Arlington Railway. On September 1, 1911, the Pacific Electric took full control over the line between Bloomington to Riverside, and built an extension north to Rialto 3.3 miles. Thus was born the Pacific Electric connection between Rialto to Riverside. On March 1, 1915, the Crescent City Railway changed its name to the Riverside, Rialto & Pacific Railroad Company and leased the Riverside Portland Cement Co. line to the Pacific Electric for operation of passenger, mail, express, and freight service.

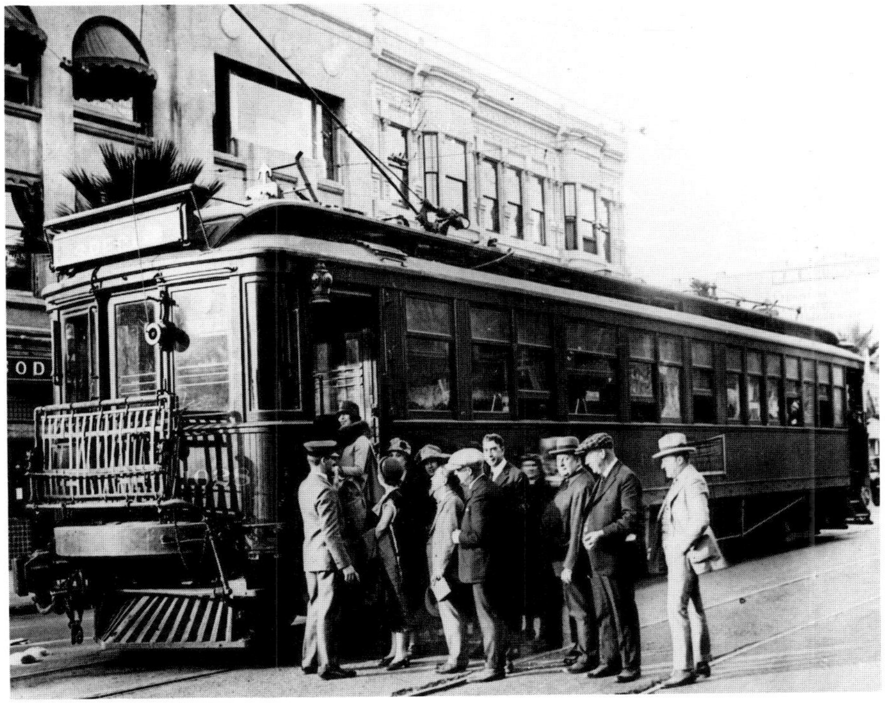

No. 1028 loads a group of passengers on the streets of Riverside, circa 1920. The uniform is not typical of the PE conductors uniform, so this would be an Orange Empire Trolley Trip excursion train. — DONALD DUKE COLLECTION

In 1940, box motor No. 1458 stops to unload express at the Riverside Portland Cement Company plant. The Union Pacific steam locomotive shed is to the right of the box motor. — BILL EVERETT COLLECTION

Union Pacific steam locomotive No. 605 is run out of its shed and is about to switch the Riverside Portland Cement Company yard. It will take a string of cement hopper cars to the Southern Pacific interchange at Bloomington. — BILL EVERETT COLLECTION

The Pacific Electric conductor waits alongside his charge, as No. 1214 prepares to take off for Los Angeles on April 17, 1939. The train is at the Pacific Electric/Southern Pacific station on Market Street. — Charles D. Savage

In the view below, box motor No. 1457 unloads its freight at the Riverside freight station, located at First and Main streets. The Pacific Motor Trucking truck, an SP subsidiary, provides pick up and delivery service. (LEFT) Box motor No. 1457 heads north on Market Street after loading its cargo at Arlington. — Both Jack Whitmeyer

The Riverside Line first saw passenger service on March 15, 1915, although the celebration was held up for sometime. A special train of Southern Pacific officials, including Chairman Julius Kruttschnitt, President William Sproule, and Pacific Electric President Paul Shoup, arrived at Colton on June 3, 1915. Two cars from the train were run down to Riverside over the rails of the once Southern California Motor Road, a steam dummy line, now a branch of the Southern Pacific. The officials were en route to check on the runaway Colorado River at Yuma. While in Riverside they participated in a ribbon cutting ceremony, and held a banquet at the Glenwood Riverside Inn, in celebration of the official start of the Los Angeles-Riverside Line which began two and one-half months earlier.

Six round trips were run daily between Los Angeles and Riverside, when first opened, and then increased to ten round trips. The Riverside car was generally attached to a San Bernardino Line train, and then cut off at Rialto. On special occasions it was a separate train. By 1926 patronage began to fall off, and then a local car was run between Riverside and Rialto at slack times, and a connection was made with San Bernardino trains. Double-truck birney car No. 106 was the local car used between Riverside and Riverside Junction (Rialto). Car No. 1036 made the last scheduled passenger run between Riverside and Los Angeles.

No. 1214 has just left the Riverside Pacific Electric/Southern Pacific station, and is photographed heading up Magnolia Street for the run to Bloomington and Rialto Junction. The Riverside Line ran on 600 volts and the power from Rialto Junction to Riverside was fine as the line was mostly downhill. In the reverse, it could be pretty week if an electric locomotive was working on the line. — CHARLES D. SAVAGE

When service between Rialto and Riverside was discontinued, city car No. 106 ran as a franchise car between the two points. — DONALD DUKE COLLECTION

The trolley wire voltage on the Riverside Line was 600 volts and supplied by the substation at Riverside. The substation at Rialto turned out 1,200 volt power for the main line. From Rialto to Riverside the line was mainly downhill and power was not a problem, however, it often was a problem when going in the opposite direction when a freight locomotive was also working on the line. The solution was to convert the Rialto to Riverside trackage to 1,200 volts. However, this would require rebuilding the overhead, build a new substation, and to convert all the local cars in Riverside to 1,200 volts. This required an expenditure of over $100,000, the PE was not willing to do this for the amount of passenger traffic on the line.

A Union Pacific steam locomotive worked the cement plant and hauled the loaded cement cars to the Southern Pacific connection at Bloomington. For cement cars destined to Pacific Electric points, these cars were picked up at Bloomington on a team track.

The hub of all Pacific Electric passenger service in Riverside was at the Pacific Electric/ Southern Pacific station on Market Street at Seventh. Riverside began in 1870 as a trade center for citrus ranchers. The navel orange was developed here in 1873. It was the first orange without seeds and had a large rind to protect the fruit. The city's showplace is the block square Mission Inn or Riverside Inn. In this scene, car No. 657 rests at the station, ready to take off for Arlington in 1937. — Charles D. Savage

Riverside-Arlington-Corona Line

A city car rolls down Market Street, bound for Arlington. In this scene, car No. 106 is at Tibbets passing track. Note the Tidewater Associated filling station at the right. I always knew it as the Flying A gasoline station. A name that no longer exists today. — Harold Stewart

The Riverside & Arlington Railway built a 6.41 mile horse car line to Arlington in 1894. The line was converted to electric traction in late 1894 as a single track line with passing tracks spaced every two miles. With the Pacific Electric under the control of the Southern Pacific, the line was extended another 8.52 miles to Corona on February 17, 1915. The SP saw lots of packing houses in the area and wished to give the Santa Fe some competition. There were few passengers between Arlington to Corona, except for citrus ranchers.

When the line first opened there were 20 trains between Riverside and Corona. By 1924 the route had been split, with 27 trains between Riverside and Arlington, and only eight trains between Arlington and Corona. By 1931 service was cut at Arlington, with 15 trains between Arlington and Riverside. All service between Riverside and Arlington was cut January 10, 1943, although freight service continued to the packing houses in Corona. At one time an extension was considered to connect Corona with the Yorba Linda Line, but this never came true.

Six hundred volt power for the line was provided by substation No. 27 at Riverside, and No. 48 at Corona. With the end of passenger service in 1943 substation No. 27 at Corona was abandoned. The line from Riverside to Corona was dieselized by 1943.

When John W. North, founder of Riverside, surveyed the city he planned for many wide streets. During the horse and buggy days this was not necessary. North loved magnolia trees and planned to line all the streets with his favorite tree. Costing $2.00 each, he gave up the idea and chose cheaper eucalyptus and pepper trees. He was unaware these trees were dirty. At the left, car No. 114 rolls south along Magnolia Avenue. (ABOVE) A Pacific Electric city car, whose shelter along Magnolia Avenue is almost hidden by a giant eucalyptus tree. Here two ladies await car No. 112, which is bound for Arlington. — Ivan Baker - Craig Rasmussen Collection

Center entrance city-suburban car No. 656 has just stopped while en route to Arlington from Riverside. The line was single track, except for the passing track at Tibbets. The conductor is on the phone to obtain a clearance to see if the track is clear. The phone box is to the left of the front end of No. 656. — Donald Duke Collection

At the left, car No. 106 waits for a run to Arlington. The station of the Pacific Electric was rather an imposing structure. Years ago, Southern Pacific local trains used this station. — HAROLD STEWART (BELOW) A one-man car, bound for Arlington, waits while the motorman/conductor walks back to re-align the switch. — DONALD DUKE COLLECTION

PACIFIC ELECTRIC COMFORT-SPEED-SAFETY

PACIFIC ELECTRIC RAILWAY POCKET TIME TABLE

San Bernardino
Riverside-Arlington
—Corona Line

San Bernardino-
Redlands Line

CORRECTED TO APRIL 1, 1928

Subject to change without notice

D. W. PONTIUS, Vice-President and Gen. Manager
O. A. SMITH, Pasenger Traffic Manager
F. L. ANNABLE, General Superintendent
Pacific Electric Bldg., Los Angeles, Calif.

Form 10 5M-3-14-28

San Bernardino, Colton, Riverside, Arlington, & Corona Line

San Bernardino to Colton, Riverside, Arlington and Corona

Leave San Bernardino Station	Leave Colton (S. P. Station)	Leave Riverside (1st and Main Sts.)	Leave Arlington	Arrive Corona
†5:10 a.m.	†5:19 a.m.	†5:37 a.m.	....	....
....	....	5:32 a.m.	5:54 a.m.	....
6:05 a.m.	6:14 a.m.	† 6:02 a.m	* 6:25 a.m.	6:42 a.m.
....	....	6:32 a.m.	6:54 a.m.	....
7:05 a.m.	7:14 a.m.	† 7:02 a.m.	† 7:24 a.m.	....
....	....	7:32 a.m.	7:55 a.m.	8:12 a.m.
8:05 a.m.	8:14 a.m.	† 8:02 a.m.	† 8:24 a.m.	....
....	....	8:32 a.m.	8:54 a.m.	....
9:05 a.m.	9:14 a.m.	9:02 a.m.	9:24 a.m.	....
....	....	9:32 a.m.	9:55 a.m.	10:12 a.m.
10:05 a.m.	10:14 a.m.	10:02 a.m.	10:24 a.m.	....
....	....	10:32 a.m.	10:54 a.m.	....
11:05 a.m.	11:14 a.m.	11:02 a.m.	11:24 a.m.	....
....	....	11:32 a.m.	11:55 a.m.	12:12 p.m.
12:05 p.m.	12:14 p.m.	12:02 p.m.	12:24 p.m.	....
....	....	12:32 p.m.	12:54 p.m.	....
1:05 p.m.	1:14 p.m.	1:02 p.m.	1:24 p.m.	....
....	....	1:32 p.m.	1:55 p.m.	2:12 p.m.
2:05 p.m.	2:14 p.m.	2:02 p.m.	2:24 p.m.	....
....	....	2:32 p.m.	2:54 p.m.	....
3:05 p.m.	3:14 p.m.	3:02 p.m.	3:24 p.m.	....
....	....	3:32 p.m.	3:55 p.m.	4:12 p.m.
4:05 p.m.	4:14 p.m.	4:02 p.m.	4:24 p.m.	....
....	....	4:32 p.m.	4:55 p.m.	5:12 p.m.
5:05 p.m.	5:14 p.m.	5:02 p.m.	5:24 p.m.	....
....	....	5:32 p.m.	5:55 p.m.	6:12 p.m.
6:05 p.m.	6:14 p.m.	6:02 p.m.	6:24 p.m.	....
....	....	6:32 p.m.	6:54 p.m.	....
7:05 p.m.	7:14 p.m.	7:02 p.m.	7:24 p.m.	....
....	....	7:32 p.m.	7:54 p.m.	....
8:05 p.m.	8:14 p.m.	8:02 p.m.	8:24 p.m.	....
....	....	8:32 p.m.	8:54 p.m.	....
9:05 p.m.	9:14 p.m.	9:02 p.m.	9:24 p.m.	....
....	....	9:32 p.m.	9:54 p.m.	....
10:05 p.m.	10:14 p.m.	10:02 p.m.	10:24 p.m.	....
11:05 p.m.	11:14 p.m.	10:32 p.m.	10:54 p.m.	....
		11:32 p.m.	11:54 p.m.	....

Corona to Arlington, Riverside, Colton and San Bernardino

Leave Corona	Leave Arlington	Leave Riverside (14th and Main Sts.)	Leave Colton (S. P. Station)	Arrive San Bernardino Station
....	....	†5:45 a.m.	†6:08 a.m.	†6:17 a.m.
....	5:59 a.m	6:23 a.m.	6:46 a.m.	6:55 a.m.
....	† 6:29 a.m	† 6:53 a.m.	....	....
7:05 a.m.	6:59 p.m.	7:23 a.m	7:46 a.m	7:55 a.m.
....	† 7:29 a.m	† 7:53 a.m	....	....
....	7:59 a.m.	8:23 a.m.	8:46 a.m.	8:55 a.m.
8:35 a.m	† 8:29 a.m.	†8:53 a.m.	....	....
....	8:59 a.m.	9:23 a.m.	9:46 a.m.	9:55 a.m.
....	9:29 a.m	9:53 a.m.	....	....
....	9:59 a.m.	10:23 a.m.	10:46 a.m.	10:55 a.m.
10:35 a.m.	10:29 a.m	10:53 a.m.	....	....
....	10:59 a.m.	11:23 a.m.	11:46 a.m.	11:55 a.m.
....	11:29 a.m.	11:53 a.m.	....	....
....	11:59 a.m.	12:23 p.m.	12:46 p.m.	12:55 p.m.
12:35 p.m.	12:29 p.m.	12:53 p.m.	....	....
....	12:59 p.m.	1:23 p.m.	1:46 p.m.	1:55 p.m.
....	1:29 p.m.	1:53 p.m.	....	....
....	1:59 p.m.	2:23 p.m.	2:46 p.m.	2:55 p.m.
2:35 p.m.	2:29 p.m.	2:53 p.m.	....	....
....	2:59 a.m.	3:23 p.m.	3:46 p.m.	3:55 p.m.
....	3:29 p.m.	3:53 p.m.	....	....
....	3:59 p.m.	4:23 p.m.	4:46 p.m.	4:55 p.m.
4:31 p.m.	4:29 p.m.	4:53 p.m.	....	....
....	4:59 p.m.	5:23 p.m.	5:46 p.m.	5:55 p.m.
5:31 p.m.	5:29 p.m.	5:53 p.m.	....	....
....	5:59 p.m.	6:23 p.m.	6:46 p.m.	6:55 p.m.
6:35 p.m.	6:29 p.m.	6:53 p.m.	....	....
....	6:59 p.m.	7:23 p.m	7:46 p.m.	7:55 p.m.
....	7:29 p.m.	7:53 p.m.	....	....
....	7:59 p.m.	8:23 p.m.	8:46 p.m.	8:55 p.m.
....	8:29 p.m.	8:53 p.m.	....	....
....	8:59 p.m.	9:23 p.m.	9:46 p.m.	9:55 p.m.
....	9:29 p.m.	9:53 p.m.	....	....
....	9:59 p.m.	10:23 p.m.	10:46 p.m.	10:55 p.m.
....	10:29 p.m.	10:53 p.m.	....	....
....	10:59 p.m.	11:23 p.m.	11:46 p.m.	11:55 p.m.
....	11:59 p.m.	12:23 a.m.	....	....

†—Daily except Sunday. *—Daily. All trains unless marked otherwise are operated daily. All trains operating from Arlington to Riverside only, will operate to 1st and Main Sts., Riverside.

Frank A. Miller's [illegible] Henry E. Huntington who formed it into his Pacific [illegible] system. In this view, Riverside & Arlington car No. 18, a single truck city trolley, operated on the Victoria Hill local line, one of three local lines. In PE days it became car No. 131. — DONALD DUKE COLLECTION

Riverside Local Lines

Riverside & Arlington Railway car No. 10 was one of several old-fashioned open cars used during the hot season in Riverside over the summer months. Some people called these cars "breesers," because of the breeze the cars created as they moved along. In 1910 the open cars were rebuilt and reconstructed into regular cars. — Donald Duke Collection

The three local lines of Riverside were a result of the merger of the four operating horse car lines to form the Riverside & Arlington Railway in 1887. Frank A. Miller, owner and operator of the famous Riverside Mission Inn put the Riverside & Arlington together, electrified the system into three lines and started service on April 5, 1899. Try as he might, he was unable to make the small system pay off. A friend of Henry E. Huntington, Miller persuaded him to buy the system and merge it into a larger operation. All the lines passed alongside the Mission Inn.

The first thing Huntington did was to upgrade the system to meet his standards. He rebuilt and double-tracked certain portions of the lines, purchased better rolling stock, and built a two-track carhouse. Alongside the carhouse he constructed a new substation. The double track section ran north and south on Main Street between First and 13th streets. The Riverside & Arlington Railway was the property of Henry E. Huntington until all his railroad assets were sold to the Southern Pacific in 1911 as a result of the "Great Merger."

The local lines in Riverside changed their route several times, and it is not important to present to the reader which street they ran on as a map is not presented. Presented is

The Riverside & Arlington began as a horse car line called the Hall's Addition Street Railway, a horse car line to a real estate development. Frank A. Miller, owner of the famous Riverside Inn, purchased the line and it was later electrified and expanded. — FIELD STUDIO

where the routes went at the last hurrah. The three routes are as follows:

Brockton Avenue Line - This line started at the center of town, at the junction of 6th and Main street, next to Mission Inn, then ran south on Main, over to Brockton, and ran south to the city limits. In 1926 this line carried 153,298 passengers, making it the most popular line. As service began to drop, Birney cars provided the service. PE asked for abandonment of the line in 1930, and was refused. It was finally abandoned June 1, 1936.

Fairmount Park-Victoria Hill Line - This line ran from Fairmount Park in the northwest part of the city, through town, to the Victoria Country Club in the south east part of Riverside. So you might say it ran from golf course to golf course. The line was built by the Riverside & Arlington Railway in 1900, and was popular, especially on weekends. Birney cars were used on the line when business fell off. The line was abandoned on March 1, 1925.

Rubidoux Line - This line was built by Henry E. Huntington in 1903 to provide transportation to the Santa Fe and Salt Lake railroad stations. It rolled west on 7th Street to Mount Rubidoux and the park. This was the only east to west route, serving the railroad station and the popular Rubidoux area. This line was abandoned July 7, 1925.

Open car No. 16 poses for the professional photographer who photographed all the rolling stock of the Riverside & Arlington Railway. This single truck car was later enclosed in. — DONALD DUKE COLLECTION

The Riverside & Arlington Railway shops rebuilt several cars, including No. 14 which was converted into this special unit. Car No. 14 contained a fancy interior, had plush seats, silk window curtains, and was painted a special color of green. The car carried President Theodore Roosevelt during his visit to Riverside. — Donald Duke Collection

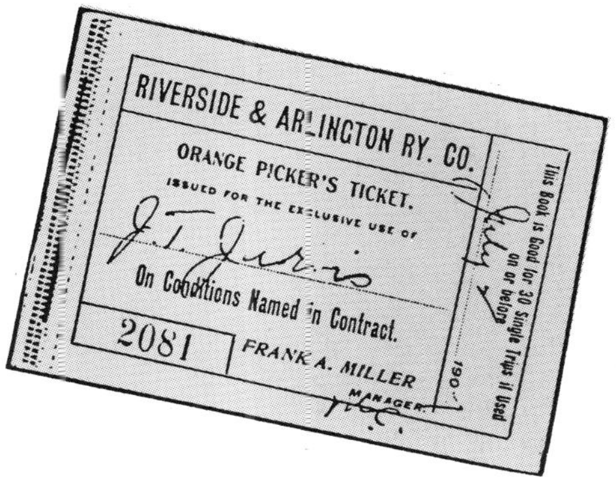

Car No. 12 was part of the original rolling stock when the line was electrified in 1899. I am sure this car did not move very fast with such tiny wheels. — Donald Duke Collection

Local car No. 101 is about to cross the Santa Fe's "Loop Line" in 1937, at Arrowhead Station on the Arrowhead-Colton Line. The metal destination sign on the front of the car says it stops at Santa Fe's San Bernardino station and Mount Vernon Avenue, while en route to Colton. The stop at Arrowhead Station was an interchange point with the Santa Fe's "Loop Line." — HAROLD STEWART

Riverside - Redlands Line via San Bernardino

Rolling west along Third Street in San Bernardino, car No. 105 is about to stop at the huge Santa Fe/Union Pacific station in San Bernardino. After letting off a few passengers, No. 105 will continue rolling west on Third Street, and then head south on Mount Vernon Avenue toward Colton. — HAROLD STEWART

The San Bernardino Valley Traction Company was an amalgamation of several horse car, and steam dummy lines. The company was formed June 8, 1901, and one of their first acts was to build a line to Colton. This 3.30 mile line was started in September 1901, and completed in March 1902. Being their first electric line, it used 600 volt for power, and was single track, with passing sidings. It was proposed to run an additional 7.68 miles to Riverside, but the line never crossed the Southern Pacific main line at Colton.

After taking over the Redlands Street Railway, a local narrow-gauge horse car line, the San Bernardino Valley Traction Company began a survey for a standard gauge line between San Bernardino and Redlands, a distance of 9.16 miles. Construction started September 3, 1901, at San Bernardino and reached Redlands during October 1902, but the electric line did not open until March 16, 1903.

At Riverside, the Riverside & Arlington Electric Railway was building an electric line north to the San Bernardino-Riverside County Line at Highgrove. At this same time, the company was electrifying its entire city system of horse car lines. Whether the San Bernardino Valley Traction Company planned to build to a connection with the Riverside & Arlington Electric Railway, or vice versa, a distance of 4.52 miles, is not known. In any case Henry E. Huntington purchased the controlling interests in both carriers in early 1903.

Nothing was done to connect San Bernardino with Riverside as far as electric traction was concerned. To pass between the two towns you rode steam trains of the Santa

Combination car No. 1300 rolls east on Rialto Avenue headed toward the San Bernardino station with a load of passengers, mail, and express from Riverside. Note that No. 1300 is followed by a Southern Pacific steam locomotive. — DON SHELBOURNE

Combination car No. 1305 has unloaded its passengers, mail, and express, and waits in the San Bernardino station in 1936 for its return to Riverside. — BILL EVERETT COLLECTION

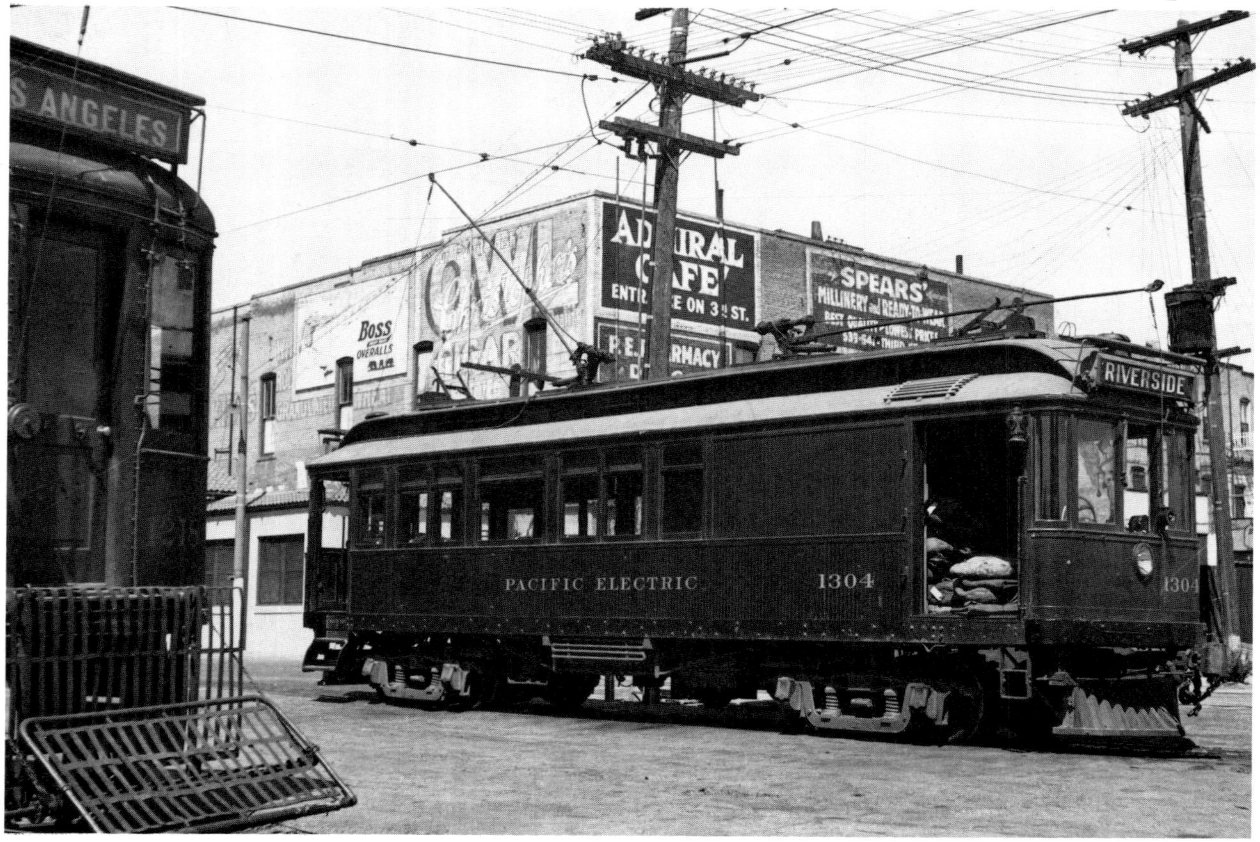

Fe or San Pedro, Los Angeles & Salt Lake Railroad. In order to solve this dilemma, the San Bernardino Inter-Urban Railway was formed in 1906 and they took over the franchise from San Bernardino to Colton, and upgraded the line. Apparently Henry E. Huntington was involved with this new company, and Henry's son Howard Huntington became vice president. After permission was obtained to cross the Southern Pacific main line at Colton, in late 1908, construction started to connect the two sections. Grading and tracklaying was slow, and in late 1910 the San Bernardino Inter-Urban Railway reached the outskirts of Riverside. After rebuilding the line into town, service began during April 1911.

In the meantime the San Bernardino Inter-Urban, the Riverside & Arlington, and the San Bernardino Valley Traction had been absorbed by Henry E. Huntington's Pacific Electric on February 15, 1911, and finally ended up with the Southern Pacific in control September 1, 1911.

Pacific Electric through service between Riverside to Redlands began in 1916 on a single track line between

The interurban is already loaded with sacks of mail, bound for Riverside. Combine No. 1304 waits for its scheduled departure from the San Bernardino station to Colton and Riverside. — DONALD DUKE COLLECTION

Bound for Colton, car No. 108 rolls westbound on Third and E streets. Note the traffic and the classic automobile which is behind No. 108 in this scene. — JEFF MOREAU COLLECTION

Riverside and San Bernardino. There were passing tracks all along the line. Sixteen trains a day, or about one each hour passed between the two cities. It was down to ten by 1927, according to the time table, and by 1935 only seven trains a day were listed. Cars made the 20.10 mile line in 50 minutes.

Service was delayed nearly all the time while trying to cross the Southern Pacific main line at Colton. The conductor had to call the Southern Pacific dispatcher and if an SP train was within 15 minutes of the cross, the PE had to wait. Once an ok was given, the conductor had to flag across seven tracks. It was much quicker by highway, and a bus line took full advantage.

On July 20, 1936 the service was down to four trains between Riverside and San Bernardino with no service to Redlands. On February 1, 1938, service was discontinued and a subsidiary Motor Transit Lines handled the bus service. There was lots of freight on the line, which often held up passenger trains. Freight service is handled in the freight section.

Rolling along a rain soaked Third Street, car No 114 is bound for Colton. — BILL EVERETT COLLECTION

(LEFT) At Southern Pacific's Colton passenger station, car No. 114 is loading lots of baggage from Southern Pacific *Golden State Limited.* Passengers had a coupon for service from Colton to San Bernardino. — JEFF MOREAU COLLECTION

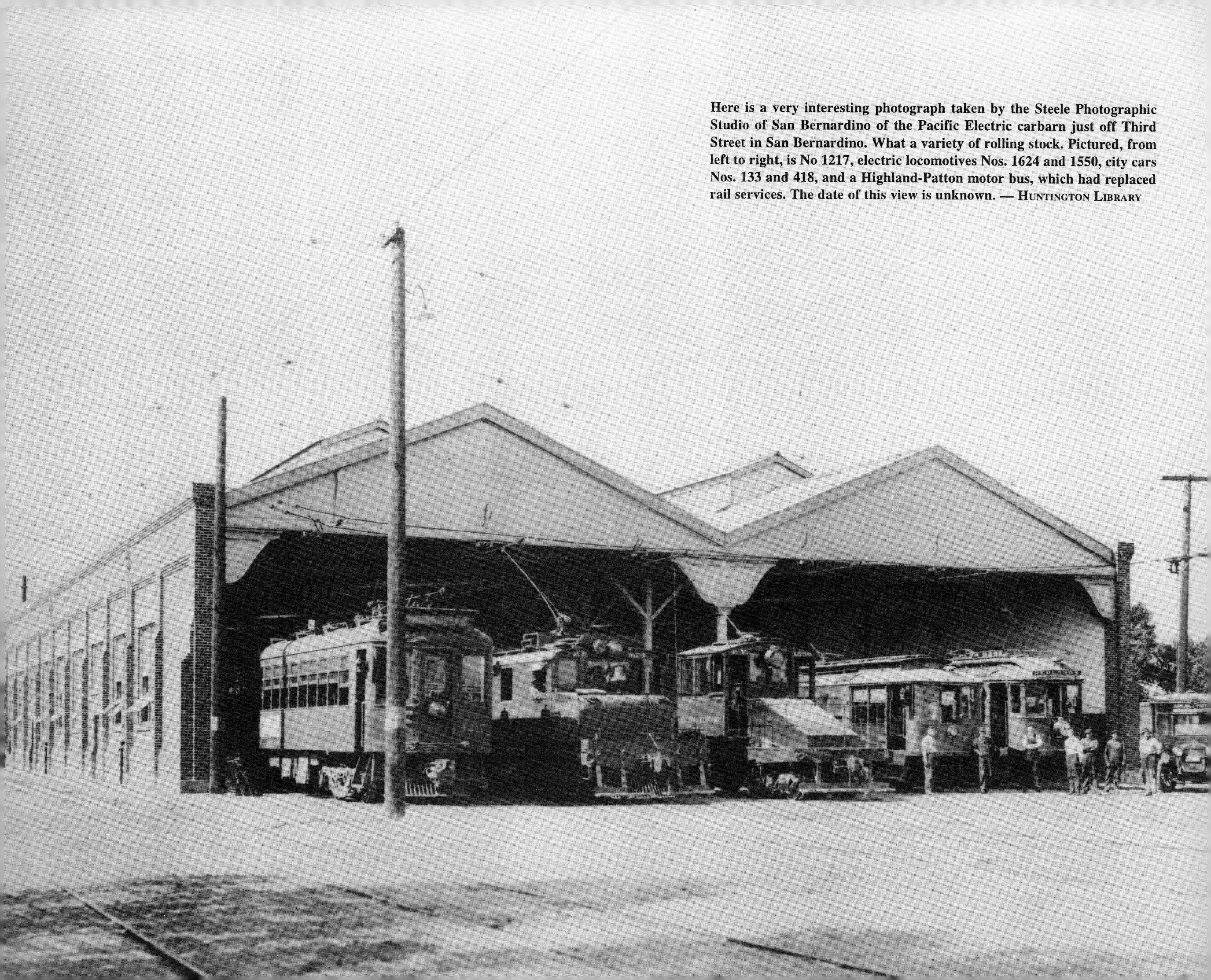

Here is a very interesting photograph taken by the Steele Photographic Studio of San Bernardino of the Pacific Electric carbarn just off Third Street in San Bernardino. What a variety of rolling stock. Pictured, from left to right, is No 1217, electric locomotives Nos. 1624 and 1550, city cars Nos. 133 and 418, and a Highland-Patton motor bus, which had replaced rail services. The date of this view is unknown. — Huntington Library

San Bernardino Local Lines

San Bernardino Valley Traction Company open-car No. 20 is about to enter the Traction Depot in San Bernardino. This car was built by the American Car Company in 1906 and carried passengers to Urbita Park. When Henry E. Huntington assumed control of the system, the car became Pacific Electric No. 38. The car carried 90 passengers, since it had no isle down the middle. — Donald Duke Collection

The following local Pacific Electric lines were operating in the San Bernardino area as a result of the "Great Merger" of 1911 and control by the Southern Pacific. Previously they were operated by the San Bernardino Valley Traction Company, a separate operation once owned by Henry E. Huntington.

Arrowhead Line - This line was built in 1901 and completed in February 1902, to run from downtown San Bernardino, almost due north to the Arrowhead Springs Hotel & Sanitarium, a rail distance of 7.25 miles.

At Arrowhead were large streams of boiling water, scalding water flowing from the rocks that seemed to indicate a never ending reservoir within the depths of the mountain. At the time the trolley line was built it was the vogue to visit these health resorts, stay overnight or for the weekend. The Arrowhead Line was a huge success when built, for there was not much else on the line except for a couple of gravel pits.

For nearly 25 years Doctor David Noble Smith treated the citizens of Southern California for consumption, which was a dreaded disease at the time. The waters were also a cure for rheumatism, dropsy, paralysis, and other chronic diseases. Since the line was all uphill, a substation was built at Arrowhead Springs in 1907 to provided sufficient power to make the climb.

In April 1903, Henry E. Huntington purchased a controlling interest in the San Bernardino Valley Traction Company, and appointed his son, Howard Huntington as president. That same year, Thaddeus Lowe, builder of the famous Mount Lowe Railway was a guest of Huntington at Arrowhead Spring Hotel. How they reached San Bernardino is not known, probably by steam train, but they rode the Arrowhead Line and took advantage of the waters at the hotel.

Freight traffic over the line increased 500 percent from 1906 to 1910 when tons of supplies of materials were shipped over the Arrowhead Line for the construction of the Arrowhead Reservoir and the dams in the mountain canyons. The San Bernardino *Times-Index* for June 27,

One of San Bernardino's horse car line was known as the City Street Railway. It was later merged into the San Bernardino Valley Traction Company. — STEELE PHOTOGRAPHIC STUDIO

San Bernardino Valley Traction Company combination open and closed car No. 9, became Pacific Electric's No. 90 when Henry E. Huntington bought the system. The car was built by the American Car Company in 1903. — DONALD DUKE COLLECTION

Pacific Electric car No. 107, a squarish California type car (half open and half closed sections) was built by the Hammond Car Company to 1900. This series of car operated in local service in Riverside and San Bernardino. — DONALD DUKE COLLECTION

1910 had this to say in regard to the Arrowhead Line. It said:

> Henry Huntington now has the Arrowhead Line on his hands which was built against judgement, and it is the main reason why the San Bernardino Valley Traction Company is not making a profit. Here is a line which cost $180,000 to build, and running to a hotel that cost $100,000, capable of caring for 80 people. Never in a thousand years will the line pay unless there is water secured in the area, and it is settled up.

Once the dams were built freight traffic dropped to near nothing, and so did the passenger service. The Pacific Electric assumed control of the San Bernardino Valley Traction Company on February 15, 1911, as a result of the "Great Merger."

The Pacific Electric extended the track a quarter mile further where the Arrowhead Water Company began to tap a spring. Arrowhead struck it rich and began hauling tank trains on a daily basis from Arrowhead Springs to Los Angeles, the location of their bottling plant. While there was a bottling plant at the spring, it was cheaper to haul the water in bulk to Los Angeles.

When Huntington controlled the Arrowhead Line, surveys were made extending the line to Lake Arrowhead. One route would have been on a seven percent grade. The route was surveyed again in Pacific Electric days according to J. B. Van Nuys, president of the Lake Arrowhead Company. Cost estimates showed that an electric railway built the whole way was out of the question.

Construction of the "Rim of the World" highway, in 1915, squelched any need for an electric line to Lake Arrowhead.

On November 30, 1931, the three scheduled runs between downtown San Bernardino to the Arrowhead Springs Hotel were given up. The only train to remain on the line was the Arrowhead Water Company tank train.

The origin of car No. 1310 remains a mystery. In 1905 this car was put through the PE shops and emerged as Pacific Electric No. 627. After the Great Merger, the car became car No. 1310. The car was placed in service on the Arrowhead Line, handling passengers, mail, and express, until 1927. — DONALD DUKE COLLECTION

Doctor David N. Smith built a sanitorium at Arrowhead Springs in 1860. It originally had few rooms. A large hotel section later was added to the original sanitorium structure. The San Bernardino Valley Traction Company built a line to the hotel, and also to the springs in 1901. The place received its name from the Arrowhead pattern on the mountain side. — DONALD DUKE COLLECTION

The Railroad Booster club of Los Angeles, ran several excursions to Arrowhead Springs. On September 11, 1939, the railroad enthusiasts ran Pacific Electric private car No. 1000 to the springs. — RALPH MELCHING

Interurban No. 1000 is at the west end on the Arrowhead Line at Arrowhead Springs in September 11, 1938. Passenger service to this point was discontinued on November 1, 1930. At the time, service only ran to Crusher, halfway on the line. — RALPH MELCHING

In 1941 the Northern California Railroad Club ran an excursion on the San Bernardino Line, including Arrowhead Springs. In this view, interurban car No. 1376 is at the end of the Arrowhead line. — STUART A. LIEBMAN

Electric locomotive No. 1591 heads up D Street from Third, with the daily load of empty Arrowhead water tank cars to be reloaded with the fresh mountain spring water. The water was taken to Los Angeles at a spur track on the four-track Long Beach Line. — JACK WHITMEYER (BELOW) The same locomotive brings down from the mountain three water tank cars of Arrowhead Crystal Springs Water. It was photographed here at 34th Street and Mountain View Avenue. — DONALD DUKE COLLECTION

The Arrowhead tank car service was dieselized in 1943. In this view, a Southern Pacific diesel, under lease to the Pacific Electric, climbs up the grade to Arrowhead Springs. — DONALD DUKE

Generally four to eight tank cars were shipped daily from the Arrowhead Water Company plant. The cars were taken to San Bernardino, then run to Los Angeles in a regular freight train. The tank cars were rather unusual. There were two large water tanks on a flat car, and the tanks were glass lined so that the water would not get contaminated. In 1958 it looked as if the fleet of tanks which were owned by the Pacific Electric would need to be replaced. Although Arrowhead received a favorable freight rate from Arrowhead Springs to Los Angeles, the cost of replacing the cars was significant. Hence it was decided to ship via tank trucks. When the last run was made is not known, or how the tank cars were disposed. In any case, the Arrowhead Line was torn up in 1960.

San Bernardino-Urbita Springs Line - This line was built by the San Bernardino Valley Traction Company to their amusement park at Urbita Springs. Also at this point was the famous Orange Show Pavilion. This single track line, with passing sidings, was extremely popular in the early days. On weekends thousands visited the Urbita Springs Amusement Park. The line ran only a long block east from the Redlands-San Bernardino-Riverside Line. On account of automobile competition, by 1927 the line was not meeting out of pocket costs and abandoned.

San Bernardino-Colton Line - This single track line was built in 1902 by the San Bernardino Valley Traction Company, to connect San Bernardino with the Southern Pacific main line which had bypassed the community by four miles years earlier. The line served downtown San Bernardino, the Santa Fe-Salt Lake depot, the large Santa Fe shops, then headed south to Colton, where it served downtown, and ended at the Southern Pacific Depot.

North D Street - Highland Avenue Line - This line was established prior to 1910 by the San Bernardino Valley Traction Company. The line ran east from downtown San Bernardino to "D" Street, then north along "D" to a terminal at Highland Avenue. Most of the line operated over the same trackage as the Arrowhead Line.

Colton-Highland Avenue Line - This line ran north from Colton to a junction with Mount Vernon Avenue and 3rd Street, then followed the same route as the above local line to Highland Avenue.

Highland-Patton Line - The San Bernardino, Arrowhead & Waterman Railroad was incorporated August 30, 1887, to build a steam dummy line from San Bernardino to Harlem Springs. The three-foot six inch narrow-gauge line was placed in operation on June 19, 1888. The company was not a financial success until an amusement park was constructed at Harlem Springs.

The same firm built a standard gauge dummy line from a junction with the San Bernardino & Redlands Railroad (a motor road), and extended the line from Harlem Springs to the newly built state hospital at Patton. All operations

Interurban No. 1300 and No. 110 are stored in the San Bernardino yard. Urbita Springs, located just south of San Bernardino, was a recreational park with things to do, picnic tables, a lake, etc. It was developed by Doctor S. C. Bogart in 1900. From 1926 to 1930, the park became known as Pickering Mineral Springs Park. After 1930 it got its old name back and was known as Urbita Springs. — ANDY PAYNE

Lots of activity at the San Bernardino Pacific Electric station on March 7, 1942. Box motor No. 1447 is ready to take off for Los Angeles, No. 112 is on a franchise run to 34th Street and Mountain View Avenue, and the other car is interurban car No. 1036, also on a franchise run. — JACK WHITMEYER

Pacific Electric birney car No. 357 rolls along Thir Street in 1939. This picture is sort of fuzzy, but the are not many birney car photographs available. The de tination sign, and the metal sign in front of the car a unreadable. — STUART A. LIEBMAN

In its last days of passenger service in the Inland Empire, a local car has just turned around at 34th Street and Mountain View Avenue. In this view, the car has just reversed ends and is ready to head back to San Bernardino. — BILL EVERETT COLLECTION

Suburban car No. 409 is loading passengers at the San Bernardino station in 1915. At this time, No. 409 was in service on the San Bernardino-Highland Line. — Donald Duke Collection (RIGHT) After the Great Merger, No. 199 of the Los Angeles Pacific Railway, became Pacific Electric No. 499. It is shown here on the Highland Line. — Andy Payne

were suspended on March 6, 1893. The road was leased to a Charles Gardner on a month to month basis during July 1894. By September 1894, Gardner became insolvent and gave up the operation. Late in 1894 the railroad was leased once again and was renamed the San Bernardino & Highland Electric Railroad by Walter Kohl. He electrified the line and built a branch off the main stem to the town of Highland.

Unable to make a profit, the San Bernardino Valley Traction Company purchased the line at auction in 1903. The SBVT upgraded the line and it was now a part of their system. When Henry E. Huntington became the principal owner of the SBVT, all lines of the SBVT were standard gauged. The Highland Line became the extension of various lines, but that end of the route was not profitable, except for freight.

The San Bernardino Valley Traction Company was absorbed in the "Great Merger" of September 1, 1911, and became part of the Pacific Electric, a Southern Pacific controlled operation.

There were eleven scheduled runs on the Highland Line in 1911, with only four direct to Patton. As the auto age advanced passenger traffic began to fall off sharply. The San Bernardino Valley Traction Company had closed

In this view, car No. 103 waits at the end of the line at Highland. City cars were used on the Highland Line during its last years of operation. This photograph was taken on November 19, 1939. — Bill Everett Collection

the Harlem Springs Amusement Park in favor of their newer park at Urbita Springs. The extension to Patton was abandoned from Harlem Springs in 1924. All passenger service was abandoned on July 20, 1936.

Tracks were taken up from Patton to Patton Junction, the turn off for the town of Highland in 1942. The line continued to experience carload freight service to the citrus plants as long as the orange trees existed.

Highland-Patton Line Power for the San Bernardino Local Lines was provided at 600 volts from substation No. 24 at San Bernardino and from No. 25 at Arrowhead. There were two substations in San Bernardino, one for 600 volts and the other producing 1,200 volts. Interurban cars of the 1000-class and 1200-class could operate over the 600 volt line, but the local cars could not operate on 1,200 volts or their motors would burn out.

I always wondered how they got all the 600 volt cars out to the Inland Empire. Harold Stewart answered my question. He said they had a slanted pit at Torrance and one at San Bernardino where they loaded and unloaded the 600 volt cars from flat cars. So equipment was not towed, the cars were taken out on flat cars.

From what I can gather, all local lines were abandoned February 22, 1942.

Redlands Local Lines

Local lines in Redlands were acquired in 1911 from Henry E. Huntington, as a result of the "Great Merger." They never were a part of Huntington's Pacific Electric until that time. Lines were of two companies. The San Bernardino Valley Traction Company operated four lines, which Huntington acquired in 1903, and one single line that belonged to the Redlands Central Railway which HEH purchased in 1908.

The Redlands lines were a losing proposition as far back as 1909. Redlands was a rather affluent town and people purchased automobiles as quickly as they appeared in showrooms. The lines were so bad money wise that they did not even make out of pocket operating costs. In 1911 the *Redlands Review* stated, "The big PE red cars are in use here. They took the place of the lousy little dinky cars in use here." What the dinky cars were I don't know, but as traffic continued to fall the PE replaced their larger cars with Birney cars (dinkys). The "Big Red Cars" also came into town as run through service from Los Angeles-San Bernardino-Redlands They also appeared on various lines as part of the Orange Empire Trolley Trip. The 1200-class cars were giants compared to the little Birney cars. At times the 600-class suburban cars with their center-entrance were used.

There was considerable refrigerator car freight on the lines due to the fact that Redlands was the center of the orange belt of the Inland Empire. There were also many packing houses not found on the Santa Fe's "Redlands Loop" line. The Southern Pacific and the Salt Lake Route (Union Pacific) turned over all their express business to the Pacific Electric, and this was served by box motors from San Bernardino.

All equipment in the Redlands, and surrounding area, ran on 600 volts. The 1200-volt line ended at San Bernardino. The Pacific Electric substation for the local lines and connections was on Citrus Street, a little east of the car barn which had been built by the San Bernardino Valley Traction Company.

Trolley No. 104, a California type car (half open and half closed) in service on one of Redlands local lines in the 1920's. — Donald Duke Collection

Former Los Angeles & Redondo Railway car in service on one of Redlands local lines following the Great Merger. — Donald Duke Collection

It is believed through interuban service between Redlands and downtown Los Angeles began in 1924. In this scene, civic officials welcome the first through car to Redlands. At San Bernardino the Redlands car was attached to the end of the San Bernardino-Los Angeles train. — Huntington Library (LEFT) City-suburban car No. 656 in service at Redlands. — Donald Duke Collection

These are the local routes that operated in Redlands. They are:

Brookside Line - This line was built in 1908, and was a single track line with passing sidings. The line was constructed by the Redlands Central Railway. This line was sold to Henry E. Huntington in 1908 and electrified. It was abandoned on June 26, 1916.

Citrus Avenue Line - This line was built by the Redlands Central Railway in 1908, the same year as the Brookside Line. This single track line was quite popular and was the first line to see Pacific Electric "Red Cars" running on it. One reason it passed through downtown and the Redlands High School which provided passengers. At times 600-class suburban center-entrance cars were used on the route. Basic power was double-truck Birney type cars. The line was one of the last Redlands route to be abandoned. It closed July 20, 1936.

County Club Line - Built by the Redlands Street Railway in 1901, a horse car system. The route only ran 2.83 miles and was single track with a couple of passing turnouts. Line was abandoned May 26, 1923.

Olive Avenue Line - The San Bernardino Valley Traction line was built in 1903. This single track line only ran 2.03 miles. It was abandoned on December 20, 1921.

Smiley Height Line - This line covered the "Silk Stocking Region" of Redlands. It ran from downtown, south to the rolling hills and was a loop line. Every other car ran around the loop in the opposite direction. This was the first local line constructed in Redlands and was built by the Redlands Street Railway. It was first run on December 10, 1899. The line was single track and used Birney single truck cars when electrified. This line was also one of the last routes to be abandoned on July 20, 1936.

All of the above routes began as horse car lines, and were later electrified. The junction of Orange, Cajon, and Citrus streets was considered the trolley triangle, and riders transferred from one line to the other at that point.

Birney car No. 331 rolls along the Smiley Heights Line during the last days of service. — Ernie Leo - Craig Rasmussen Collection

Birney car No. 328 at Cajon Street at the junction of Citrus and Orange streets, in Redlands. The date is July 1933. — Ivan Baker - Craig Rasmussen Collection

Sunday, July 20, 1936, was the last day of service on the Smiley Heights Line. Here a group of well-wishers celebrate the last car. — Ernie Leo - Craig Rasmussen Collection

Box motor No. 1451 rolls eastbound, during 1939, along Rialto Avenue while en route to the San Bernardino freight house with a load of less-than-carload freight, and express. No 1451 has just crossed the Santa Fe's "Short Line" crossing. The semaphore signal protects this crossing. — CHARLES D. SAVAGE

Box Motor Service

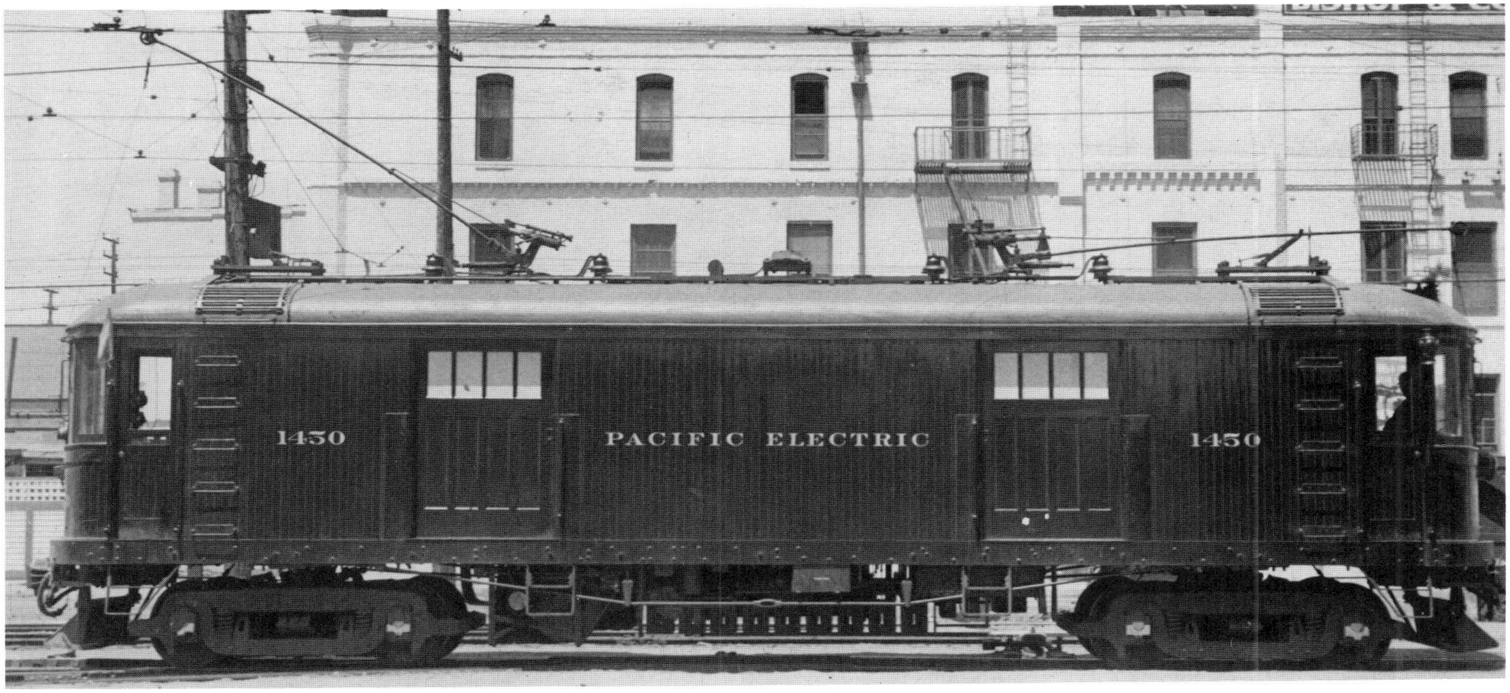

The first car of the 1450-series box motors as it appeared at the Pacific Electric's Seventh and Central shops in 1917. Two years later, for some unknown reason, this car was rebuilt into wrecker No. 002. This series was all built in 1915. All of this series was also able to operate on either 600 or 1200 volts. — Donald Duke Collection

One of the most common forms of interurban freight service was the handling of package freight, express, current metropolitan newspapers, and sack mail carried by box motor. Samuel Moffett said in *McClures Magazine*, in 1903, that "Electric freight is as flexible as an elephant's trunk, and is adept of picking up and carrying little things."

The almost universal workhorse of the interurban was the "box motor." It was a motorized single unit electric railway baggage car that could carry mail, express, or less-than-carload freight. It had large sliding doors on each side for handling the movement of freight in and out of the car. Box motors were fast, flexible, and several schedules could be run in a single day. They did such a good job that they literally stole express delivery away from the steam roads. In fact they handled most of Southern Pacific's express business in Southern California.

From the earliest days of the Pacific Electric, box motors handled this service. On the Eastern Division, when it was still a 600 volt line, box motors took peeping chicks, and parcels to Covina and Pomona. Pacific Electric's 1400-class were express cars and Railway Post Office cars. Each car had a standard coupler and were able to handle one or more box cars if an electric locomotive was not available. Centers for box motor loading and unloading was at the back of the Pacific Electric headquarters building at 6th and Los Angeles Street. Another point was Central Station on Central Avenue at 5th Street, and later at Los Angeles Union Passenger Terminal which had four terminal tracks.

When the San Bernardino Line opened to 1,200 volts of DC power, this limited the box motors that could be used on the line. Box motors Nos. 1451-1456 could operate on 600 or 1 200 volts and were built in the Pacific Electric Torrance shops patterned after the successful motors Nos. 1430-1444 which were built by PE in 1905 and 1910 to operate at only 600 volts. When the Southern Pacific gave up its suburban service out of Portland, Oregon in 1927, cars Nos. 1445-1449 came to the Pacific Electric. These were 47-foot steel express cars with porthole windows in the ends. They ran on 1,500 volts in Portland, but when the PE got them they were switched to 600-1,200 volts DC.

Photographed in 1941, box-motor No. 1456 rolls along the Crestmore Branch of the Union Pacific en route to PE's right of way. The motor has in tow a wooden Southern Pacific box car. On the siding are two flat cars of large poles. — Jack Whitmeyer

The cars became the workhorse of the San Bernardino Line.

When box motors were running, their crews were assigned from the passenger roster, not from freight crews. Box motor work was a cushion job as schedules were not rigid. At stations or freight houses that had their own crews, box motor crews did not have to load and unload their cars. Box motor service flourished for many years, despite the constantly multiplying horde of trucks and the ever growing network of good roads and freeways.

The Pacific Electric never got into non-motorized trailer cars which were handled by box motors. Very few western roads got into this type of operation. Only the hardiest interurban line survived the Depression unless they had a system of express delivery and interline freight exchange with steam roads.

Sack mail, limited express, and current metropolitan newspapers were often carried aboard regular passenger runs. Such parcels were carried in the motorman's compartment and he would hand down the sack mail or express to waiting hands. Late edition newspapers were handled in bundles. The PE sold stickers that could be attached to the bundle as prepaid stickers in a booklet. Time and truck competition caught up with PE's box motor service in Southern California. All service ended November 15, 1952.

At Riverside, No. 1451 leaves the Riverside Freight House on Orange Street, and then will head for San Bernardino. The conductor has just lined the switch in this 1942 scene. — Jack Whitmeyer

A box motor is traveling north along La Cadena Drive in Riverside, during 1941, on the present site of the I-215 freeway. Note both the motorman and the conductor in the front windows of No. 1455. — Jack Whitmeyer

Rolling over Main Street on a grade separation at Riverside, No. 1453 is on its way to San Bernardino with a load of packages and Railway Express. Note that you can see the motorman at the controls of his charge. — Jack Whitmeyer (BELOW) For lots of freight and newspapers, the Pacific Electric sold script books for bundles of freight and newspapers . For newspapers an example is shown below. They were issued in bundles of 5, 10, 20, and 100 newspapers. — Frank Newton Collection

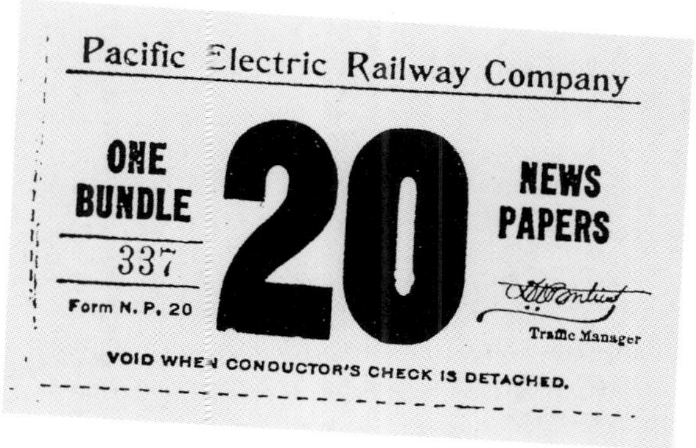
Pacific Electric Railway Company

ONE BUNDLE 20 NEWS PAPERS

337

Form N. P. 20

Traffic Manager

VOID WHEN CONDUCTOR'S CHECK IS DETACHED.

The front end of Pacific Electric's box motors was handsome and impressive. The 1450-class were built in Pacific Electric's shops. They had standard couplers, a steel underframe, and footboards for the crew to ride on during switching. — Donald Duke

Rolling along Market Street, in Riverside, No. 1457 has just passed Seventh Street in this 1942 scene. This motor was originally a former car on the Portland, Eugene & Eastern Railway, a Southern Pacific subsidiary. The car was built by Pullman in 1920. — JACK WHITMEYER

A box motor rolls eastward along the former Southern Pacific branch line which was later electrified. This scene is at La Verne, and the station is of typical Southern Pacific design. — Ivan Baker - Craig Rasmussen Collection

Rolling westbound at Fontana station, No. 1457 has just unloaded its cargo for Fontana, then moved to the end of the passing track to wait for an eastbound passenger car. — Ivan Baker - Craig Rasmussen Collection

Bound for San Bernardino, No. 1457 rolls north along La Cadena Drive, at Russell Street, in Riverside in 1942. This car is a former Portland, Eugene & Eastern Railway passenger car converted to a Box Motor. The car saw regular service at Riverside. — Jack Whitmeyer

Box motor No. 1458 approaches Rialto Avenue in San Bernardino, while en route to the freight station. No. 1458 is another PE&E car which was formerly a passenger car and rebuilt into a box motor at Pacific Electric's Torrance shops in 1937. — Charles D. Savage

In former Oregon days, No. 1449 was one of five express motors which was run on the Portland, Eugene & Eastern Railway. In this scene, No. 1449 works its way toward Los Angeles after crossing the Southern Pacific main line at El Monte. — Charles D. Savage

During the early 1930's, finds several box motors at the United States Terminal Annex at Central Station, at Fifth Street in Los Angeles. Central Station was the Southern Pacific/Union Pacific station before the opening of Los Angeles Union Passenger Terminal. — Bill Everett Collection

Just after the opening of Los Angeles Union Passenger Terminal in 1939, finds several box motors at the Pacific Electric freight terminal. In this view finds Nos. 1448, 1359 (a former combine car), and No. 1446. — Charles D. Savage

Just east of El Monte, in 1947, finds No. 1449 en route to Los Angeles Union Passenger Terminal. Two ladies thought this was the regular passenger car from Baldwin Park to Los Angeles. — CHARLES D. SAVAGE (BELOW) No. 1448 waits on South Main Street in Colton for Southern Pacific's Nos. 4104 and 5038 to complete their wye movement across the Pacific Electric tracks. — JACK WHITMEYER

Box motor No. 1447 clears the Claremont station, in 1944, bound for Los Angeles. Note the hood over the headlight, which all cars used during the war to keep stray light from shooting into the sky. — IVAN BAKER - CRAIG RASMUSSEN COLLECTION

The Pacific Electric operated Railway Post Office trains between 1905 and 1950. This was a record among interurban railroads. The interior of an RPO car was just like cars on main line railroads. The clerks sorted mail into sacks while en route, and then picked up and dropped off sack mail at various stations. The Pacific Electric did not pick up mail on the fly as was done on main line railroads. The Railway Post Office route between Los Angeles and San Bernardino was inaugurated on September 2, 1947, and ended July 13, 1950. In this scene, train No. 502 is about to leave the Rialto station bound for Los Angeles. — JACK WHITMEYER

Railway Post Office Service

Los Angeles to San Bernardino

Two San Bernardino and Los Angeles Railway Post Office mail cars work their way between San Bernardino and Los Angeles (Los Angeles Union Passenger Terminal) on August 10, 1948, as train No. 502. Jack Whitmeyer photographed the westbound train at Bench. The Bench passing siding is to the left of the main track. This is where passenger trains used to pass in the good old days. — JACK WHITMEYER

When direct passenger service began between Los Angeles and San Bernardino on July 11, 1914, the Railway Mail Service of the United States Post Office established closed pouch service to communities along the line. The reason for this route was to provide quicker mail service to towns. Such mail sacks where either carried in the motorman's compartment or by a Railway Post Office car where clerks sorted mail, and dropped and picked up sacks along the route. On a R.P.O. car, it had a mail slot, just like the mail drop on the corner, where a letter could be posted.

The Post Office Department established the Pacific Electric's terminal headquarters at their 6th and Main Terminal for mail handling. R.P.O. cars gathered at ground level just off Los Angeles Street and underneath the elevated structure. Here mail cars were dispatched all over the system. Mail came to 6th and Main from Southern Pacific's Arcade Station, and later Southern Pacific-Union Pacific at Central Station. In later years the incoming and outgoing terminal was at Los Angeles Union Passenger Terminal.

Here Post Office transfer clerks loaded cars with sacks. Mail pouches were dropped off and picked up all along the line. The R.P.O. cars had the mail slot on the side of the car. If someone dropped a letter into the slot it would be worked as the car moved along. If a letter was dropped in the slot at Baldwin Park for Claremont, it would be sorted and dropped off at Claremont. Mail destined for points beyond the cars route, it was sacked for Santa Fe, South-

Westbound mail train with RPO car No. 1406 on the point, and mail storage car No. 1458, exchanges mail pouches at Fontana in 1946. The stake truck took the mail direct to the Fontana Post Office. (LEFT) Mail train with Nos. 1406 and 1448, rolls along Rialto Avenue in San Bernardino just west of J Street. — Both Jack Whitmeyer

A busy scene at the San Bernardino station. Since the passenger trains had been taken off, the only thing available was the bus. Passengers mill around waiting for the next bus to Los Angeles. Los Angeles bound RPO car No. 1406 is loading sack mail which can not be seen in this picture. When loaded it will take off and stop en route at various stations. This scene was taken on December 20, 1947. (LEFT) Mail train No. 502, with Nos. 1407-1448, rolls through a cut approaching the Meridian Avenue overpass in San Bernardino. — Both Jack Whitmeyer ern Pacific or Union Pacific mail trains, and dropped off at exchange points. The clerks working mail in the R.P.O. cars were Postal employees and carried a gun, as they handled Registered Mail. Only the train crew were Pacific Electric employees.

Since the San Bernardino Line was 1,200 volts only four cars could be used. These cars came to the Pacific Electric secondhand from the Portland, Eugene & Eastern Railway, Southern Pacific's Portland, Oregon, operation. The cars originally operated at 1,500 volts, but were converted to 600 and 1,200 volts and received Nos. 1404-1407. The R.P.O. cars were acquired in 1928 and were distinguished with porthole windows in their ends.

The last Railway Post Office route on the Pacific Electric was established on September 2, 1947. This run left Los Angeles Union Passenger Terminal at 12:45 P.M., and three hours later reached San Bernardino. The car left San Bernardino at 4:40 P.M. and returned to Union Station at 7:50 P.M. This also happened to be the last interurban R.P.O. service on any system in the U.S.A., to start and the last to end. It finally surrendered to a Highway Post Office on September 18, 1947.

This photo shows that you can post a letter on the side of a Pacific Electric Railway Post Office car. The slot was high, and could not be reached by a midget. In this view, Jack Whitmeyer's wife posts a letter. — Jack Whitmeyer

With downtown San Bernardino looming in the background, mail train No. 502 pulls out of the station and takes the main track to Rialto Avenue. RPO No. 1406 and mail storage car No. 1445, will make lots of stops while on its run to Los Angeles. Note the postal clerk in the doorway, the express clerk was in the second car. All Jack Whitmeyer's views are of the westbound runs, the reason was that the sun was in the right direction. — Jack Whitmeyer

Mail train headed by No. 1406 skips along as it crosses the concrete viaduct over Lytle Creek just west of San Bernardino. The date is August 17, 1948. — Jack Whitmeyer

Steel steeple cab locomotives Nos. 1601-1618 were built by the combination of Baldwin-Westinghouse between 1912-1920. These locomotives enabled the PE to engage in the freight business at steam road standards. Nos. 1619-1631 were added to the roster between 1924 and 1925. They were designed as Class D. In this scene, Nos. 1620 and 1630 work a long westbound freight at the Southern Pacific crossing at El Monte in 1947. — Donald Duke

Freight Service

This photograph finds two Pacific Electric locomotives, Nos. 1619 and 1627, waiting for the hi-ball at the interchange track at Colton. The freight will take-off for San Bernardino, and on to Los Angeles. In the background is Colton's Southern Pacific shops and ice loading facilities for refrigerator cars. The date is July 12, 1947. — JACK WHITMEYER

Although the major portion of income derived by the Pacific Electric in the early years was the transportation of passengers, freight be came an important part of their transportation facilities. Freight started out small with "power cars" which were little more than a powered flat car with a cab in the center of the car. Freight grew and grew, until at the end it provided the major income for the Pacific Electric.

In 1903 the Pacific Electric inaugurated freight service, and by 1909, it was big business and grew 77 percent that year. By 1921 freight provided 24 percent of the company's total income. Being that the PE covered the Southland like spider webs, it became the first interurban in the State of California to cooperate with the steam railroads for interchanging of freight, and to issue joint tariffs for every kind of commodity all across the United States. At the time PE had some 1,200 box cars in the interchange pool. After the "Great Merger of 1911" and the takeover by the Southern Pacific, the PE became the major feeder for the Southern Pacific in the Southland.

Under the influence of the Southern Pacific, the PE established freight houses, a freight solicitation department, and handled both carload and less-than-carload freight. It worked industrial sidings, encouraged industry to build plants and factories on line, and sought out the citrus industry which was big business at the time. It handled current newspaper delivery, railway express, and carried sack mail. Freight on the PE was handled on the system in three ways. They were:

1. Carload freight to interchange with steam railroads.
2. Less-than-carload freight, Railway Express, and sack mail handled by box motor.
3. Current daily newspapers, sack mail to a specific town were handled in the front end of passenger equipment.

In Henry E. Huntington days, freight was handled by little more than a "power car" with a cab in the middle of a flat car. Several of these were built in the PE shops at 7th and Central. The motors were able to handle a box car or two, work an industrial siding, and take the freight to an interchange point. None of these crude and powerless freight motors ever operated in the Eastern Division when it was a 600 volt line. An additional nine wood steeple cab

Electric Motor Power Car No. 1526 was acquired by the Pacific Electric as a result of the Great Merger in 1911. Built by the Los Angeles Pacific in 1906, motors Nos. 1526-1529 were assigned to the Riverside and San Bernardino areas to work the sidings of the Orange Empire, until replaced with larger electric locomotives. — Donald Duke Collection

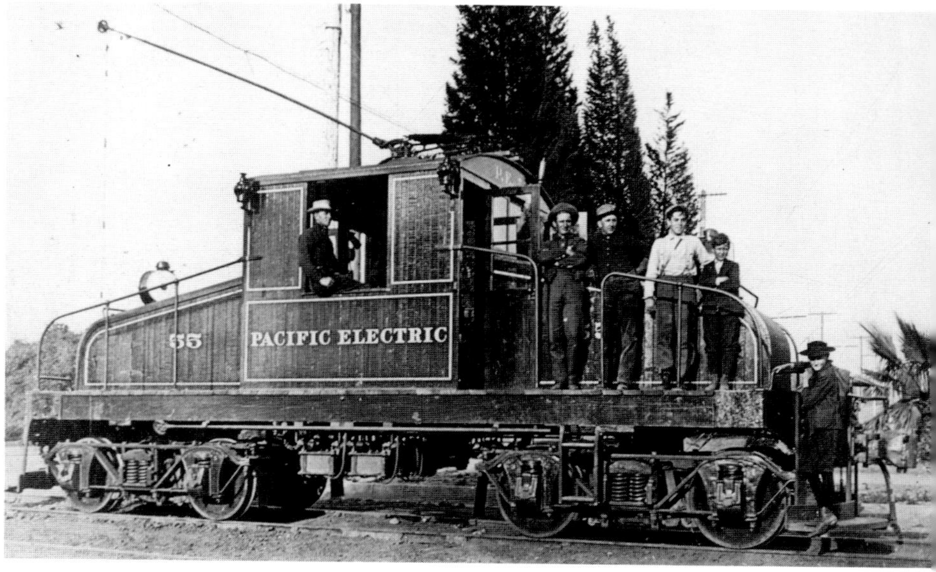

The Pacific Electric built four wooden electric locomotives in its shops in 1908 complete with steel underframes. They were numbered Nos. 54-57. The locomotives were meant for switching in the Southern Division and the Inland Empire. No 55 became No. 1560 long before the San Bernardino Line was completed. — Donald Duke Collection

locomotives were built in the PE shops in 1909. They were a lot more powerful, and could have worked the packing houses on the Covina Line. Covina was a huge citrus point for the San Gabriel Valley.

Beginning in 1905 there was a great debate between the City of Los Angeles and the Pacific Electric in regard to the moving of freight over city streets. Mayor McAleer had a PE train arrested as it worked from the Northern Division to the Southern Division, over San Pedro Street. Henry E. Huntington himself got into the fight. He carried a lot of influence in Southern California and was able to contact a businessman who got to the mayor. As a result Mayor McAleer backed off and the PE was permitted to run freights on city streets between 10:00 P.M. and 5:00 A.M. It was also brought out that the Southern Pacific main line ran on Alameda Street, and trains passed day and night to Arcade, then Central Station at the end of Fifth street. Before the merger, the volume of freight handled continued to climb. Requiring more power, the PE shops built two steel steeple cab electric locomotives, Nos. 1599-1600. The No. 1599 weighed 113,700 lbs, and the 1600 weighed 103,300 lbs, and each one could out pull anything else on the line. As a result of the merger, the PE acquired a variety of wooden electric locomotives, nothing as big as Nos. 1599-1600.

In the meantime, the Baldwin Locomotive Works had combined with Westinghouse Electric to build some large electric locomotives for interurban service. Baldwin would build the body of the locomotive and Westinghouse would supply all the electric appliances. The Baldwin-Westinghouse team's first trial tested their power in small box cab units. Finding many blind spots for switching, they next experimented with a steeple cab design in four classes. The biggest and most powerful were the Class D of 60-ton weight. They could pull 60 empty freight cars, the same as a 4-8-2 type steam locomotive. They had four Westinghouse motors of 200 hp. each, and were able to pull a load of 1,250 tons. They had multiple-unit control, and were capable of operating on 600 or 1,200 volts. They were the most powerful locomotives built for interurban service.

In 1912 the Southern Pacific Company ordered several for their Southern Pacific operations in Portland, Oregon, the San Francisco Bay operation, the Peninsular Railway, and the Pacific Electric. Those units on the PE were Nos., 1601-1618 and painted red in color. They were first put in service October 30, 1912. They were magnificent machines.

The big Baldwin-Westinghouse locomotives were placed all over the system, especially in the Southern Division which handled Long Beach, San Pedro, Santa Ana, and Redondo Beach freight. Several were located at State Street Yard, east of Macy Street Yard which was mostly used for storage of passenger equipment. State Street Yard was the assembly point for freight on the Northern and the Eastern Division. Several 1600-class locomotives were placed at San Bernardino to handle switching citrus packing plants, and work trains between San Bernardino and State Street Yard. In 1924 the PE purchased 1,350 additional freight cars to be used in interline service. With these cars available, the PE became the third largest car-

Operating in the streets just east of downtown Redlands, No. 1619 has just picked up a refrigerator car of citrus and is taking it to Colton for icing. — Donald Duke

Electric locomotive No. 1616 hauls a single car of smudge pot oil near Upland. Smudge pots were used to keep citrus warm during freezing nights. — Donald Duke Collection

No. 1625 works its way toward San Bernardino with a string of refreigerator cars and a tank car. The freight cars will be interchanged at San Bernardino or Colton. — Bill Everett Collection

No. 1590 was photographed switching in the State Street Yard, assembling a train bound for San Bernardino and Colton. No. 1590 was destined for Cuba, however, unable to pay for it, the PE purchased it at a bargain price in 1920. The motor was capable of operating on either 600 or 1,200 volts. — DONALD DUKE

The No. 1631 was also switching in the State Street Yard. The crewman holding on to the trolley cord was known as the "trolley pup." It was his job to see that the wheel was on the wire either moving backwards or forwards. — DONALD DUKE

rier in point of volume of freight in California.

In the 1920's most through freights between State Street Yard and San Bernardino were operated by one 1600-class locomotive on the point, and one at the rear. The rear locomotive would be cut off along the line to handle local switching. As freight volume continued to rise, and passenger volume fell, 13 additional electric locomotives were required. With the Torrance Shops geared to build anything, it was decided to build the locomotive bodies and frames in PE's own shops. Hence in 1924 and 1925 the Torrance Shops turned out 13 electric locomotives, just like the Baldwin-Westinghouse units under license. These were equipped with four General Electric 205 horsepower motors against 225 horsepower for the 1601-1618 class, however, these units were 3,000 pounds heavier. The 1619-1631 class were regulars on the San Bernardino Line.

In 1922 the franchise to run freight on San Pedro Street was about to expire and the PE asked for an extension. There were several plants located on San Pedro Street or nearby which required service. Westinghouse Electric

Electric locomotives were restricted from downtown Los Angeles streets between 9:00 P.M. and 5:00 A.M., except during World War II. Here motor No. 1609 works toward the Southern Division from the Northern Division. It is shown here at Sixth and San Pedro Street. — BILL EVERETT COLLECTION

A long mixed freight is seen leaving San Bernardino, bound for State Street Yard in Los Angeles. It was photographed here crossing over one of the lead tracks of the Santa Fe, into their "B" yard, and precooler area. The long drag is handled by Nos. 1624 and 1622. These "juice jacks" were originally painted PE red, however, during the war they were painted black with white strips on each end. — Donald Duke

Not all the bridges and viaducts west of San Bernardino were constructed of concrete. This heavy steel viaduct crosses over the lead tracks in Santa Fe's "B" yard. Motors Nos. 1630 and 1620 clatter across the steel bridge. (RIGHT) No. 1628 and 1620 work an eastbound freight through Baldwin Park. The Baldwin Park passenger station is at the right. — Both Bill Everett Collection came to the rescue when they told the city if we can't build on San Pedro Street we will take our business elsewhere. An extension was granted to run on the streets at night, and also to run locomotives in transfer from one yard to another during the daytime. They issued a 21 year franchise and limited operations from 7:00 P.M. to 7:00 A.M.

In due course, on account of the volume of freight, freight was transferred to the Southern Pacific at State Street Yard for transferring freight cars down the east side of the Los Angeles River to a transfer point near Butte Street Yard on the Southern Division.

In post World War I years, the San Bernardino Line experienced dynamic growth all along the line. The bulk of freight was citrus, agricultural products, rock and gravel, bunker oil in tank cars which was used for smudge pots used to keep orange and citrus trees warm during a freeze, consumer goods and lumber. As the Depression approached traffic reached a status quo as the motor truck came on the scene. To fight this inroad, in 1929 the Pacific Electric instituted door-to-door pick up and delivery service for less-then-carload freight. Winning back a lot of lost customers, freight was kept at par.

The Depression was to effect both freight and passenger service. During this period many marginal services were discontinued, and money losing branches were taken up. Passenger services were cut and many local lines were abandoned. In fact, during this time, it was freight that kept the Pacific Electric from going under like most interurban lines across the nation. There was an increase in the export of agricultural products which kept the rails shining on the San Bernardino Line. The Pacific Electric was dying as an interurban line, and was becoming a commuter railroad with freight service. In 1935 freight began to pick up and was nearly back to pre-Depression days by 1938. As war clouds loomed on the horizon, PE's freight traffic soared.

No United States interurban line played a greater role in World War II freight and passenger traffic as did South-

A southbound double-headed freight, with Nos. 1619 and 1630 on the head end, cross the Southern Pacific east-west main line at Ninth and J Streets in Colton bound for Riverside. The dispatcher will not clear this crossing if a Southern Pacific train is within 15 minutes of the crossing. — Jack Whitmeyer

Nos. 1619 and 1631 are seen leaving Colton's Pacific Electric Colton Yard, bound for San Bernardino. Southern Pacific's Colton Yard is seen in the background. — Donald Duke

A westbound mixed freight works its way westbound in 1951 at the Eastern Avenue overpass in Los Angeles. — FRED MATTHEWS - CRAIG RASMUSSEN COLLECTION

Rolling along Badillo Avenue in Covina in 1946, a westbound freight, with Nos. 1631-1628, rolls by the Covina station. Note the unconcerned motorist at the right. — NORMAN NEWCOMB - CRAIG RASMUSSEN COLLECTION

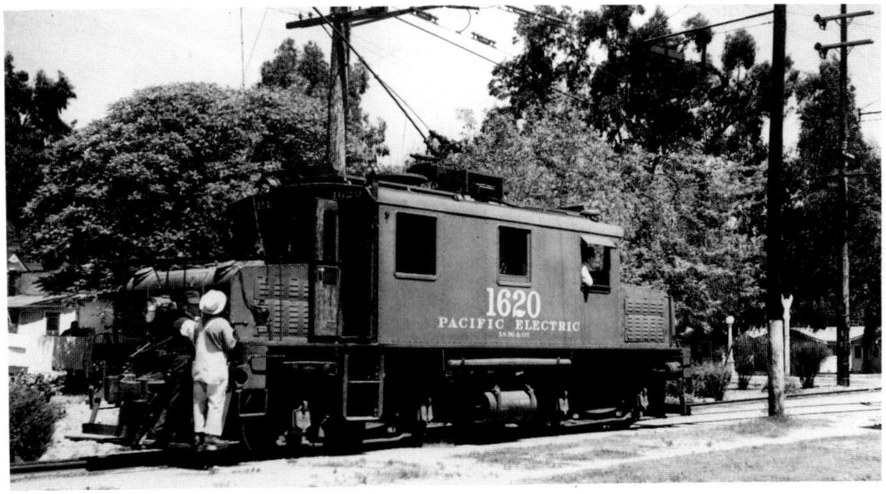

At Rialto, No. 1620 was seen switching a spur off the main line. The brakeman and "trolley pup" are riding the rear footboards. — CHARLES D. SAVAGE

Shortly after taking out the double-track between Baldwin Park and Valley Junction for construction of the San Bernardino Freeway, Nos. 1625 and 1627 roll eastbound along Ramona Avenue in South Alhambra. — IVAN BAKER - CRAIG RASMUSSEN COLLECTION

Bill Barham, a Pacific Electric freight conductor on the San Bernardino Line, got the idea of producing a photographic essay about the use of steam in combination with electric locomotives. So Barham, Donald Duke, and Frank Peterson covered the scene over several weekends, between State Street Yard and San Bernardino/Colton. The article appeared in *Trains Magazine* on May 1946. In this scene, Southern Pacific locomotives No. 1740, and Pacific Electric motor No. 1625, roll a 20-car freight eastbound just east of Etiwanda. This area was loaded with vineyards. — Frank Peterson - Donald Duke Collection

Steam on the San Bernardino Line

Another eastbound freight, with Southern Pacific No. 1817 and PE motor No. 1629, moves east across the San Gabriel River trestle. Although not much water passes below in summer, it could be a raging torrent when it rains during the winter. Although block signals work on a track circuit, the wig wag crossing signals work off the overhead. So it was imparative an electric locomotive had to be a part of the consist. — Donald Duke

Southern Pacific locomotives Nos. 1774 and 1817, plus PE motor No. 1616 pause at Baldwin Park for orders. It was a perfect opportunity for Bill Barham to get out his camera and to take a picture. (RIGHT) In this scene, Bill captured the crew as the trainmaster hands up the orders to the fireman of No. 1774. At Baldwin Park the freight will take off on the Southern Pacific branch north of Covina. — Both Bill Barham

ern California's Pacific Electric Railway. Considered the largest interurban system in North America, the PE provided a transportation framework for much of the development of the Los Angeles area.

At the beginning of World War II, Southern Pacific's main line between Los Angeles and Colton became jammed with traffic. The line was single track with limited passing sidings, and all kinds of spurs east of Los Angeles that fed lumber yards, and light industry. The Pacific Electric's San Bernardino Line came to the rescue and became a second main line between Los Angeles and Colton.

The PE also faced a dilemma. They did not have enough electric locomotives to handle the traffic. The Southern Pacific came to the rescue with 2-6-0's, 2-8-0's, 4-6-0's to assist. Electric locomotives had to be used since all crossing wig-wags were operated from an overhead contact. So it would be an electric-steam freight train. The common practice was to double-head with a steam engine on the point, followed by an electric locomotive or two. The steam was cut off at San Bernardino on a Los Angeles-Colton run. Steam helpers were used between Baldwin Park and Alta Loma after oil and water facilities were established at Baldwin Park.

The PE right-of-way operated on several blocks of city streets as it passed through Covina. Residents began to complain of the noise and the smoke from the steam locomotives passing through several times a day. The approach to Covina from the west was on a three percent grade, so steam locomotives were working hard as they rolled east through Covina with lots of smoke pouring from the stack. The City of Covina issued a protest which did not reach deaf ears. Southern Pacific's branch to Pomona skirted the north part of Covina, away from the residential area. The branch took off from the Southern Pacific main line at Bassett, east of Baldwin Park, and ended up in Pomona. There were no overhead wires over the western portion of the line, so electric locomotive trolley poles had to be pulled down on this non-electrified section. SP's staff system protected trains between Bassett and Lone Hill, where the PE overhead returned. The steam-electric freights operated all the way to San Bernardino where the steam was cut off. Electric locomotives took the freights to the interchange at Colton. Some of the freight trains were 50 cars long between Los Angeles State Street Yard and Colton.

Steam locomotives were not new to the Pacific Electric. They were used in the construction of lines, and used on non-electrified trackage. They appeared mostly on the Southern Division at Long Beach, San Pedro, and Redondo

Train operation over Southern Pacific's Covina Branch was operated by the ancient staff system. There were five pairs of machines on the line. A close look at one of these machines, reveals a long curved groove consisting from 15 to 20 steel pins. These are the staffs. Before a train enters a staff operated section, the conductor works the pins up through the groove to the top of the box. If the track ahead is clear, the pins will stay and will start to roll down by turning the dial. This locks the machine, and also sets the machine at the other portion of the track to be covered. The train then rolls over the cleared section of track. At the other end, the conductor releases the section traveled by turning the dial and the pins fall down, and then sets the machine ahead. Why block signals were never installed remains a mystery. — Frank Peterson - Donald Duke Collection

At Baldwin Park, in 1945, an eastbound freight crosses over the Pacific Electric double track and heads east over the former Southern Pacific branch line running north of Covina. No. 1740 and Pacific Electric motor 1626 head the freight. Why the brakeman is riding the footboard is a mystery. (BELOW) On the day this photograph was made, Covina seemed to be the gathering place of steam locomotives. Nos. 1774 and 1796 are working a freight to San Bernardino, and No. 2823 is doing switching duties. — Both Donald Duke

A long mixed freight steams just outside of San Dimas behind Southern Pacific steamer No. 1740 and Pacific Electric motor No. 1625. The trolley pup seems to be riding the back platform of No. 1625, but does not have control of the trolley cord. Must be out catching a breath of fresh air. — Frank Peterson

Beach lines. Dur ng the war they were used on the Glendora Line, Gardena L ne to San Pedro, and even on the Newport Beach Line. The Pacific Electric was a partner with the steam roads of the Harbor Belt Line. Pacific Electric steam locomotives under lease were used in this service as well.

Steam locomotives were attached to freight trains at State Street Yard, just east of Macy Street Yard. From State Street, steam ran all the way to San Bernardino. A waiver was received from the City of San Bernardino to use steam locomotives on city paved streets to the yard. Here the PE interchanged with the Santa Fe and the Union Pacific. Since the yard and lines in the area were 600 volt, many of the wood and light electric locomotives serviced industries and citrus packing houses.

The Pacific Electric purchased the Southern Pacific Covina Branch on September 1, 1946 for $400,000. The line was only electrified from Vineland (Baldwin Park) to Lone Hill and opened November 4, 1946. The section of the line from Vineland (Baldwin Park) to Bassett was never electrified. In using the line during World War II, the usual operation of steam/electric was to have the steam locomotives haul the electric motor dead westbound (downgrade) from Lone Hill to Baldwin Park. Eastbound steam/electric

At La Rica, midway between El Monte and Covina, finds box motor No. 1446 taking Southern Pacific No. 1724 in tow. Where they are taking the steam engine is anyone's guess. The date of this scene is 1947. — Harold Stewart

While en route to visit Aunt Edna, in 1944, my father saw the wig wag swinging at Euclid Avenue, in Ontario, and we stopped for a westbound freight with Southern Pacific No. 1714 and Pacific Electric motor No. 1630. This photo was taken with a 127 Plastic Brownie Camera. — Donald Duke

freight (upgrade) used the PE line from Baldwin Park to Lone Hill so the electric locomotives could be used. In effect it became a double-track operation to and from Lone Hill.

Freight east and west of State Street Yard was handled by the Southern Pacific which picked up loads at State Street and transferred it down or south along the banks of the Los Angeles River to Butte Street Yard on PE's Southern Division. Northbound traffic was picked up at State Street Yard and taken to Taylor Yard for all Northern California-Oregon-Washington freight. Very little switching was accomplished at State Street Yard except for freight destined for the Northern Division.

After the war things returned to normal, and steam locomotives on the San Bernardino Line were discontinued.

Freight traffic exploded following World War II. The populace who had done without during the war years, and with money in their pockets, wanted new homes, refrigerators, and washing machines. Pacific Electric freight trains carried sand and gravel, lumber, cement, and consumer goods. Citrus trees were ripped out from Covina east through Redlands and Riverside as new housing tracts were built. The trucking industry also boomed and stole a lot of PE's short haul traffic. Without the packing houses, the citrus groves at Redlands, Riverside, and Corona, and

How would you like to see a westbound freight on the Pacific Electric in San Bernardino come charging at you? Well, here you will see a wartime drag on Rialto Avenue with Southern Pacific No. 1917 and Pacific Electric No. 1625 speeding under the 1200 volt catenary overhead. — Donald Duke

A 62-car freight is working its way eastbound at La Verne. The train, behind Southern Pacific Nos. 1774 and 1796, and Pacific Electric motor No. 1621 is moving at 40 m.p.h. The surrounding area was once a lush orange grove. — Frank Peterson

Diesels on the San Bernardino Line

Pacific Electric diesel No. 5241, under lease from the Southern Pacific, switches sidings at El Monte. Note the trolley pole is up to work the wig wag signals. — IVAN BAKER - CRAIG RASMUSSEN COLLECTION

A diesel powered Pacific Electric freight crosses the Southern Pacific main line at El Monte. The train is westbound. Note the trolley poles installed on the diesel to set the crossing signals. (RIGHT) A General Electric diesel runs light toward Los Angeles after passing under the Eastern Avenue crossing. — IVAN BAKER - CRAIG RASMUSSEN COLLECTION

Crossing the San Gabriel River, east of El Monte, Pacific Electric diesel No. 5212 is photographed rolling westbound. Note that none of the trolley poles are up to work the crossing wig wags. — IVAN BAKER - CRAIG RASMUSSEN COLLECTION

other locations in the Inland Empire were abandoned. Except for interchange freight with the Union Pacific and Santa Fe, about all that was left was the Arrowhead water train.

Then came the era of freeway building. This swept the San Bernardino Line in one fell-swoop starting with the Aliso Street trackage and the abandonment of the entire Northern and Eastern Division. State Street Yard and the San Bernardino Line was used as an alternative route for the Southern Pacific between State Street Yard and El Monte. This part of the line is used by Metrolink as part of its Los Angeles to San Bernardino Line and Amtrack sometimes uses the line with its *Sunset Limited* when the Alhambra main line is busy. The former Pomona Line of the Southern Pacific is owned by the Metropolitan Transit Authority and leased to Metrolink.

The old Pacific Electric main line east of El Monte to San Bernardino was abandoned.

Railroad Enthusiast Excursions

Excursions on the Pacific Electric was big business, especially on Saturday and Sundays. On Sunday, September 14, 1938, the Railroad Boosters ran a trip to Riverside and San Bernardino. The car of choice this day was the private and parlor car No. 1000. In this view the railfans inspect car No. 656, a 1200-class car, etc. — RALPH MELCHING

A three-car train was run for the Railroad Boosters in June 1941 to Riverside and San Bernardino. Nearly 120 fans compete with camera, railroad hat, and jacket with patches all over of other railroads pause at Tibbets passing siding at Riverside for a local car to pass. — RALPH MELCHING

The same June 1941 excursion train stops at Rialto to fix the trolley pole on No. 1375. Note the rear pole is also down. The fans chose an "Orange Empire Trolley trip" sign for the trip. — Stuart A. Liebman

The outbound Railroad Boosters excursion train makes a stop at Upland. The fans jump out to inspect the station. — Ralph Melching

The Railroad Booster special excursion train included a run to Redlands. In this scene, No. 1375 makes a run across the Santa Ana River bridge between San Bernardino and Redlands, at La Quinto stop for the camera fans. — Ralph Melching

The June 1941 excursion train pulls up to the Colton station of the Southern Pacific, and waits for the passing of a steam train headed east. The conductor of the excursion train stands next to the crossing to wait for the SP train to pass. — Stuart A. Liebman

On the return trip to Los Angeles, the Railroad Boosters special is about to pull into a passing siding west of Glen Ellen, for an eastbound train — Stuart A. Liebman

Bibliography

Books

Baldwin Locomotive Works. 1923. *History of the Baldwin Locomotive Works.* Philadelphia: Baldwin Locomotive Works.

Daggett, Stuart. 1922. *History of the Southern Pacific.* New York: Ronald Press.

Evans, Gerinda W. 1954. *Collis Potter Huntington.* (Volumes One and Two). Newport News. Mariner's Museum.

Fredericks, William B. 1992. *Henry E. Huntington and the Creation of Southern California.* Columbus: Ohio State University Press.

General Electric. 1912. *The Direct Current Railway - 1,200 volts.* Schenectady: General Electric Company

Hofsommer, Don L. 1986. *The Southern Pacific 1901-1985.* College Station: Texas A&M University Press.

Kennan, George. 1922. *E. H. Harriman.* (Volumes One and Two). New York: Houghton Miffin Company.

Middleton, William D. 1983. *Traction Classics: The Interurbans.* San Marino: Golden West Books.

Middleton, William D. 1985. *Traction Classics: Interurban Freight.* San Marino: Golden West Books.

Pacific Electric Railway. 1914. *Corporate History of the Pacific Electric Railway.* Los Angeles: Pacific Electric Railway.

Swett, Ira L. 1962. *The Riverside & Arlington Railway.* Los Angeles: Ira Swett Books.

____________________. 1964. *Cars of the Pacific Electric.* Los Angeles: Interurban Press.

____________________. 1964. *The Pacific Electric in Pomona.* Los Angeles: Interurban Press.

____________________. 1976. *Lines of the Pacific Electric - Northern & Eastern Divisions.* Los Angeles: Interurban Press.

____________________. 1978. *Cars of the Pacific Electric - Volume III - Locomotives and Non-Revenue Cars.* Glendale: Interurban Press.

Thorpe, James. 1994. *Henry Edwards Huntington.* Berkeley: University of California Press.

Westinghouse Electric & Manufacturing Co. 1925. *Baldwin-Westinghouse Electric Locomotives.* Pittsburgh: East Publishing Co.

Manuscripts – Magazine Articles

Crossley, Rod. "Pacific Electric R.P.O. Service 1900-1950." *SP Trainline,* Spring 2001, pp. 24-30.

Donovan, Frank P. "Pacific Electric." *Trains Magazine.* June 1941. pp. 10-31.

Duke, Donald. "Pacific Electric Railway: An album of Electric Railroading." *Pacific Railway Journal.* 1958. pp. 51-63.

Middleton, William D. "Electric Fast Freight." *Railroad History.* Volume 151, 1984. pp. 16-69.

Rasmussen, Craig, and Flynn, Jack. "The Pacific Electric Goes to War – Moving Freight." *Pacific Electric Historical Society.* Monograph No. 4, 2000.

"The Pacific Electric Opens a New Line." *Railway Age.* July 25, 1914, p. 163.

Whitmayer, John L. "Rememberances of the Pacific Electric." *Pacific Electric Historical Society.* Monograph No. 2, 1999.

Acknowledgments

This is the second volume, of a four book series, featuring the routes and operating divisions of the Pacific Electric Railway. The Eastern Division was without a doubt the most diverse of the four operating divisions. It had the longest routes, the best of interurban passenger equipment, and experienced box motor and freight traffic. The route extended due east from Los Angeles into the heart of the citrus and wine belt of Southern California.

While the Pacific Electric was organized by Henry E. Huntington in 1901, very little of the Eastern Division existed while Huntington remained in the picture, except for the line to Covina, and local lines in Pomona, Riverside, San Bernardino, and Redlands. Most of the Eastern Division was formed by the Southern Pacific when they took control of the system, as a result of the Great Merger of Southern California interurban routes.

The San Bernardino Line was built to high-speed standards. The main line operated on 1,200 volts of direct-current power. Branch lines extended to Pomona and Riverside, but were operated at 600 volts of power. When built, the entire Eastern Division was not heavily populated, except for the towns of Pomona, Riverside, and San Bernardino. The region was primarily farm land, orchards, and vineyards.

Surprisingly, not many photographs exist of when the Eastern Division was built. It was not until a group of railroad enthusiasts ascended on the Pacific Electric, with camera in hand, that photographs began to appear.

For the variety and richness of the illustrations presented in this volume, I am grateful to individuals and organizations. Many of the photographers whose pictures appear in this book are now deceased. Prints exist in the hands of collectors, historical societies and railroad organizations. The photographs of Bill Barham, Ernest Leo, Stuart A. Liebman, Frank Peterson, Charles D. Savage, Don Shelburne, Robert Slocum, and the Steele Photo Studio are among them.

To those photographers and collections still with us, I give thanks to Bill Everett, the Huntington Library, Ralph Melching, the Jeff Moreau Collection, Frank Q. Newton, Mike Patris, Andy Payne, the Craig Rasmussen Collection, and Harold Stewart.

I am especially grateful to Jack Whitmeyer of Redondo Beach, who photographed the box motors, electric freights, the Railway Post Office service on weekends and days off while working full time for the Santa Fe Railway in San Bernardino.